Strategies for Stay-at-Home Parents

by Kristine Berggren

 **Meadowbrook Press**

Distributed by Simon & Schuster
New York

Library of Congress Cataloging-in-Publication Data

Berggren, Kristine.
   Strategies for stay-at-home parents / by Kristine Berggren.
     p. cm.
   Includes bibliographical references and index.
    ISBN 0-88166-435-9 (Meadowbrook) ISBN 0-684-02020-3 (Simon & Schuster)
    1. Parents--Life skills guides. 2. Homemakers--Life skills guides.
    3. Parenting. 4. Child rearing. I. Title.
   HQ755.8.B473 2003
   649'.1--dc21

                                                      2003009961

Editorial Director: Christine Zuchora-Walske
Proofreaders: Joseph Gredler, Megan McGinnis, Angela Wiechmann
Production Manager: Paul Woods
Graphic Design Manager: Tamara Peterson
Art Director: Peggy Bates
Typesetting: Sheryl Thornberg
Index: Beverlee Day

Copyright © 2003 by Kristine Berggren

All rights reserved. No part of this book may be reproduced or transmitted
in any form or by any means, electronic or mechanical, including photo-
copying, recording, or using any information storage and retrieval system,
without written permission from the publisher, except in the case of brief
quotations embodied in critical articles and reviews.

Published by Meadowbrook Press, 5451 Smetana Drive, Minnetonka,
Minnesota 55343

www.meadowbrookpress.com

BOOK TRADE DISTRIBUTION by Simon & Schuster, a division of Simon
and Schuster, Inc., 1230 Avenue of the Americas, New York, New York 10020

07 06 05 04 03   8 7 6 5 4 3 2 1

Printed in the United States of America

Dedication

This book is dedicated to the memory of my mother, Kathryn Frey Berggren, who passed on to me the value of the written word *and* the value of being a mother.

Acknowledgments

The first order of business is to thank my wonderful, patient, and precise editor, Christine Zuchora-Walske. She wrestled with the often rather raw material I sent her, rendering it sensible and presentable—and, I hope, enjoyable to read.

I also want to thank the friends, parents, and writers who read and critiqued an early draft of the book and offered many useful suggestions: Darcy Bell-Myers, Jennifer Britz, Jane Davidson, Beverlee Day, Alex Dietz, Mary Heer-Forsberg, Rob and Maureen Fuhr, Alison Haseman, Marcy Kempner, Rachel Morris, Kristin Nelson, Anne Neuberger, Nanci Olesen, Kelly O'Rourke, John Rosengren, Patty Schmitz, and Sarah Sponheim. Patty Schmitz helped give form to the financial worksheet included here, and John Truckenbrod of First Advisors Financial Services offered a great deal of valuable feedback. I am most grateful for all the parents, some my friends and some interviewed specifically for this book, with whom I've spent countless hours at coffee shops, on park benches, at kitchen tables, on living room floors, or on the telephone talking about this subject that matters to us so deeply: how our parenting choices both reflect our values and help us retain our values. I hope you can hear their voices as you read these pages.

My family of origin and my husband's family of origin have been so excited and supportive about this project—both the parenting part of it and the book part of it. I send a big hug to my dad, Dick Berggren, who has *always* believed in me; and to my husband's parents, Ben and Rita Olk, whose love for me and support for my family make all the bad in-law jokes you ever heard dead wrong.

Finally, this book quite literally would not have been written without several people, the first being Ben, my husband and father of my children. His joyful partnership and coparenting have undoubtedly made me a better mother. The others are my three children, Ben, Kari, and Betsy. I'm grateful to them for revealing the sparkle in their young eyes, for asking the questions that get me thinking, and for knowing how to love what they love, to rephrase the poet Mary Oliver. Mostly I thank them for the privilege of learning how to love them.

Contents

Introduction

Stay-at-Home Parenting in the Twenty-First Century

You have a job. You have a baby. After your parental leave is up, you find someone else to care for your baby so you can go back to your job. That's what most people do, right?

Actually, there is another option: staying home with your child. Many parents do return to their jobs for personal or financial reasons, but many others prefer to work out a way to be at home with their children for a few months, a few years, or more. Various factors affect how parents approach this decision: their careers, temperaments, finances, values, and overall family dynamics. And over time, any one of these factors can shift, causing parents to reevaluate whether to work or to stay home—or who stays home and who works outside the home.

This book is designed to help you consider your options—and, if you think staying home will work for your family, to develop a plan for making the transition. It raises important questions about what staying home means financially, emotionally, and careerwise; tells stories of mothers and fathers who have chosen to stay home for several months to several years; and examines the practical aspects of at-home parenting as well as the feelings parents have about staying home.

My Story of Heading for Home

I've been working on this endeavor called motherhood for more than a decade now. It's a project without a finish date; once you're a parent, your job is never entirely done. Ironically, it's also a project with many deadlines; it's full of daily—if not hourly—tasks like doing laundry, cooking meals, taking naps, changing diapers, kissing owies, organizing play dates, running errands, soothing little sorrows, finding big fun.

I planned to stay home from the time my first-born was conceived; I never even pretended it was a tough choice. I had no student loans or other big debts besides a mortgage. I had a spouse with a job (though we certainly weren't "rolling in the bucks," as my high school friends and I used to describe wealthy families we knew); my husband was a middle-school history teacher. I hadn't invested time and money in postgraduate work or paid my dues in a profession on my way up a career ladder. I was a jill-of-all-trades: I'd done some social work, volunteer organization, journalism—even worked at a daycare center for several months.

That short-lived job providing child care isn't listed on my résumé anymore, but it's meant more than meets the eye. It gave me big clues about what it's like to leave your child in someone else's care every day and about the reality that many daycare centers hire people who are living and breathing and don't have criminal records—but who don't necessarily know much about raising children. I resolved to stay home with my kids because I knew too much.

I want to make it clear that I don't think substitute caregivers are inherently bad. Clearly, some child-care providers can and do provide high-quality care. But the overall quality of daycare in this country is a concern to many parents and child advocacy organizations. Hazards range from being plugged in to TV for too many hours to being ignored as individuals by overwhelmed and undertrained staff to being unable to form attachments because caregivers come and go so frequently. (It's worth noting that children in their parents' charge may face some of the same disadvantages. Merely having an at-home parent is not a panacea for all that is wrong with child rearing in this country today.)

A year after our second child was born, my husband and I realized his salary as a teacher wasn't enough, so I found a part-time job and a home-based daycare I thought we could live with. (It turned out to be far less satisfactory than I had anticipated, but that's another story.) I continued to work three days a week until my third child was born. I asked my boss for a job share to minimize the time away from my new baby, and I got it. When my daughter was about a year old, I quit my job to try free-lance writing, a path I'd always wanted to follow. It turns out that a home-based mix of mother work and writing work suits me best. Though my circuitous career path doesn't make for a blue-chip résumé, it does give me freedom to keep all my work—parenting and writing—in balance.

Strategies for Stay-at-Home Parents

This book is designed to help you define the parenting experience you want to have. You research everything else you buy or do—vacations, mortgages, cars, schools—so it also makes sense to research what it takes to stay home with your kids. Consider this a starting point for your studies.

Other books about parenting, such as Ann Crittenden's *The Price of Motherhood,* Sarah Blaffer Hrdy's *Mother Nature,* and Jon and Myla Kabat-Zinn's *Everyday Blessings: The Inner Work of Mindful Parenting,* discuss the work of parenting from economic, sociobiological, and spiritual standpoints. I incorporate those perspectives into this book, but its main purpose is to articulate the value of at-home parenting without presuming it's the right choice for every family.

People choose at-home parenting for many reasons: to avoid the anxiety and expense of making child-care arrangements, because one spouse earns enough for the whole family, because they want to homeschool their children, because of religious or cultural values that dictate an at-home parent, or simply because they believe they are the best qualified to raise their children and want to be with them. There are also many reasons people do not or cannot choose at-home parenting: commitment to a career path, inability to live on one income, the need to retain a job with medical insurance or other benefits, single parenthood, moving from welfare to work and being required to procure paid employment, and personal satisfaction from working outside the home.

The heated discussion about why and how women stay home to raise children while foregoing income-producing work tends to flare up for a while, then smolder—but the spark is never doused entirely. True feminism allows each woman to choose any line of work, yet choosing the traditional work of raising one's children is tricky because it flies in the face of other goals: equal pay for equal work, breaking the glass ceiling, and debunking sexist myths about women's capabilities. But feminism also has to be about what is good for women and their children—and for many women that's creating lives centered in their own homes.

The decision to have an at-home parent is not necessarily about a mother sacrificing her career to be a housewife. Instead, it's about what works for the whole family. As Brenda, a Memphis at-home mother of three, puts it, "For us it was a family decision, not an individual decision." She and her husband have a solid relationship, they'd waited seven years to have children, and he has far greater income-earning potential in his career as an investment banker than she has as a social worker. "You never know," acknowledges Brenda, "but right now it's working out."

Even when the stay-at-home arrangement looks traditional (that is, the stay-at-home parent is mom), today's at-home parent is no June Cleaver. Moms at home are much less likely to consider themselves housewives than their mothers probably did. They care far less about their kitchen floors than about their families' well-being. And many couples today are comfortable deciding that diaper duty and car-pooling can be dad's primary responsibility, or that two parents who tag-team score the best deal of all: no child-care costs, equal responsibility for the emotional and practical aspects of caring for their children, and the benefits of two incomes. Chapter 1: The Choice looks at each of these possibilities.

Some books about stay-at-home parenting assume it's a mother's preordained (even divinely ordained) job to stay home to raise her child. This book presumes that who stays home is open for discussion. Other books presume economic privilege that relatively few families enjoy. At-home parenting does require a certain amount of privilege; for example, very few single parents can make the choice to stay home. But it doesn't require wealth. This book offers many examples of families who aren't wealthy; most are somewhere in the middle class.

Since money is such an important factor in the at-home parenting equation, Chapter 2: Money Matters walks you through the transition from two incomes to one, shows you how smart planning can get you over the bumps with your relationship and bank account intact, and helps you minimize the risk of losing retirement income for the partner at home. It also includes ideas about generating income at home or through part-time work.

Although this book is not a comprehensive guide to child rearing, it does discuss some practical parenting issues at-home parents face that differ from those of parents who work outside the home. When you choose at-home parenting, your workplace is the sandbox, the kitchen, the laundry room—anywhere your kids are. How does that affect you and your family? Chapter 3: Caring for Your Child covers the basics of life with kids, such as nutrition, sleep, discipline, fun, and learning, from the perspective of an at-home parent. From diapers to driver's licenses, from nap time to nightly curfews, Chapter 3 discusses how to foster independence and competence in your child from babyhood through adolescence and how to nurture your own parenting confidence by learning about your child's development.

And what about your needs? Some parents report they didn't know how strongly they would feel about their babies and find they're more satisfied than they'd anticipated with life as at-home parents. Others struggle mightily with creating structure and meaning in their life at home and with having very little downtime—no coffee breaks, no lunches out, no sitting down to a quiet desk or methodically working through a to-do list.

At-home parents also require the support of friends, family, and especially their partners. In fact, agreement between the at-home parent and the employed parent on the value of at-home parenting is critical to its success. Finally, just about every at-home parent I interviewed for this book said, "Make sure you tell them to find time to be alone sometimes!" Coping with the needs of others day in and day out requires time-outs (for you, not your child)! Chapter 4: Caring for You takes an honest look at these issues and suggests dozens of tried-and-true strategies for keeping your sanity and finding time for self-care as you adjust to new expectations and integrate your new identity into your existing sense of self.

Chapter 5: Nitty-Gritty touches on the practical and organizational matters at-home parents—indeed, all parents—wrestle with. This chapter is a wide-ranging but by no means exhaustive look at the dirty details of life at home with a child. When you become a parent, life turns upside down for a time, and your definition of "normal" changes forever. This chapter offers tips for handling the changes, simplifying your life, and enjoying a child's-eye view of the world. It covers cutting down clutter, getting a handle on cleaning, and managing time and information effectively and efficiently. It also encourages you to establish egalitarian roles that help you and your partner manage your household as a unified team.

Most parents return to the paid work force at some point. Chapter 6: Everything Changes offers strategies for keeping your finger in the pie and explains why it pays off, in the midst of your family-focused life, to carve out a parcel of time to stay connected to your profession and keep your skills sharp. In this chapter you can read about when and how other at-home parents have made the transition to employment and learn how to step back in to your professional groove when the time comes.

There is not, and never has been, a single right way to raise children. Biology is not destiny for women—or men, for that matter—and we must all adapt to our particular circumstances and do the best we can with the resources at hand. But our sociobiological makeup as species homo sapiens does dictate that our children are born just about helpless and in need of constant attention, assistance, and guidance to grow to physical, mental, and social maturity. So the question really is *Who is or are the best candidate(s) for the job of raising your child to maturity? And How do you balance that formidable task with the reality of gathering enough nuts and berries to feed your family and find a cave in which to take shelter from the cold? And How can you find the emotional and material support you need to do both?* These are complicated questions for individuals and society to ponder and answer. This book will help readers see that it is not only possible but perhaps desirable to find those answers in the home zone.

Chapter 1

The Choice

Many Voices

If you've picked up this book, chances are you're a stay-at-home parent or you're seriously thinking about becoming one. You may have strong opinions about this issue, or you may feel ambivalent. Whatever your stance, I want you to know that I'm not digging trenches in the "mommy wars" (the ongoing and often bitter debate between some parents who work outside the home and others who stay home with their kids). Rather, I'm here to tell you that staying home with your kids can be a great choice. But it's not necessarily an easy choice.

The quotes and stories offered on pages 2–5 reflect a wide variety of perspectives on the choice to stay home. Some of these parents stayed home for just a few precious months with their newborns. Others worked for years before quitting to be at home with older kids. Some made the move when they had second children. Others knew they'd be home right from the start. Though they all are—or were—stay-at-home parents, their stories give a glimpse of the many reasons parents head for home and the different challenges they face.

At-Home Parents Describe Their Decision-Making

"Monetarily I can't justify daycare for three children. Also, I want to be with them as much as possible during these formative years. My husband and I feel that giving up fancy dinners out, shopping trips, and expensive vacations has been well worth it to be our children's primary caregivers."

—*Jennifer Lankford*
Lawrenceville, Georgia

"I was thirty-nine, and it was my only chance to be home with my kid. [After my divorce] I said I wanted to work weekends. I was firm about it. He's my only one, and I really want to enjoy him."

—*Maria Rubinstein*
Minneapolis, Minnesota

"We decided before we had kids that I would stay home. I had job flexibility. Plus, my wife was dedicated to her careeer and climbing the corporate ladder. We didn't want to put our children in daycare."

—*Bob Franks*
Chicago, Illinois

Four Real-Life Decisions

Learning to Live Lean

Heidi is an energetic, outgoing woman who provided computer networking support for an advertising and marketing company before she became a mother. She and her husband, Tim, fully expected Heidi to return to work after Jackson was born, but the idea of placing her child in daycare didn't sit right with her—partly because she recalled her own bad experiences as a daycare kid.

As Jackson's birth approached, Heidi and Tim researched the cost of daycare in their area and found that it was about $750 to $800 per month. Then they tallied the cost of Heidi's commute, including gas, car insurance, and upkeep, and looked at how they spent their disposable income. After comparing the overall financial and emotional costs and benefits of having both parents working and Jackson in daycare, they found a way to tighten their belts so Heidi could be home. To accomplish that in high-rent San Jose, California, they took these steps:

- Tim changed jobs and got a significant salary increase, and they began to put money away immediately.
- They cut down on socializing with friends in bars and restaurants, which alone saved them hundreds of dollars a month.
- They sold one of their two cars.
- They eliminated most travel.

"[The routine of daycare and work] just got repetitive. I think I said to myself, 'Is this it? Is this a family life?' They're only young once."
—*Jean Ng*
Concord, California

"I didn't feel very nurtured by my mother. Staying home with my kids and giving them what I didn't get helped me with my issues from the past. I wanted to care for them and know every single thing they ate and did, be the one that knew them the best."
—*Kristy Dean*
Davis, California

"I'm not sure how we decided. We wanted someone to be home. Secretly I was hoping it would be me. John was more hireable."
—*Leslie Abadie*
Madison, Wisconsin

"My husband was in school until the baby was nine months old. I had to work full-time until then. My daycare provider saw a lot of the "firsts"—I felt I had missed out. I couldn't wait to stay home when my husband got his first job."
—*Suzanne Borchers*
Vancouver, Washington

"I figured since I make the higher income, I'd be the one to work. I always wanted to have a parent home. I even looked for a spouse with that in mind; I never wanted to marry another doctor! It makes my life easier. I feel better about where my kids are."
—*Julie Brady*
Colorado Springs, Colorado

Heidi says, "It's definitely tough sometimes. We can't do all the things we want to do. But that's okay because we're with Jackson." She also misses the stimulation of being out in the marketplace, but says being with her son is worth the temporary sacrifice.

"It's personally rewarding in a way I couldn't have predicted," Heidi concludes. "[It's easy to] forget about your own childhood and how free you felt. It's almost like you feel you're in his shoes...it brings out the child in yourself. For me, that's really rewarding."

Creating a Calm Center

Mary Dee Hicks earned a six-figure salary as a senior vice president at an international consulting firm where she'd worked for fifteen years. She and a colleague did speaking tours, wrote books and curriculum for corporations, ran workshops—all in all, a seventy-hour-a-week job. "I was embedded in the fabric of the institution," she says.

Deciding to quit her job was difficult. "It was such an integral part of my identity to be a professional woman with expertise, and people were paying me for it." But ultimately, she couldn't deny that she was barely "keeping tensions in check between how much home demanded and how much work demanded. The costs became more vivid than the payoffs."

The costs included a growing sense that her son and daughter, then nine and eleven, needed a quality of attention their long-time nanny couldn't provide. "She was devoted, but she wasn't running the household and relating to the kids the way I would. The kids required a different kind of finesse and judgment," says Mary Dee. "I was always compromising [my time with] them. There was not one big crisis moment, but lots of little things. They would say things like, 'Why do you have to go to Houston?' or 'Why are they more important than me?'"

Mary Dee also found herself gazing out the window of her twentieth-floor office in downtown Minneapolis on sunny days, imagining the nanny walking the family dog through a local park. She notes wryly that she later wrote an essay titled "How My Dog Ruined My Career."

Finances were not an issue for Mary Dee and her family, and she admits "it was an incredible luxury to be able to decide this way." Leaving her job has allowed her to pursue personal interests such as piano and gardening. Being home has also benefited her family. "It's a lot better in subtle ways. My anxiety and distraction are way down. The juggling act is simplified," she says. "I'm more available. The household feels more centered and calm."

Despite the rewards, Mary Dee still struggles with her identity as someone who used to have a business card reading "Mary Dee Hicks, Vice President". She now calls herself a "civilian" mom. But she asserts that her parenting style hasn't changed: "I've always seen myself as an intuitive, nurturing parent who wants my children to be who they are and pursue their dreams. If I'm creating a safer, calmer launching pad for them now, all the better."

Small Sacrifices

Jane, mother of a six-year-old boy and four-year-old girl, worked full-time as a personal banker in Denver until two years ago, when her daycare situation changed. That was the excuse she was looking for to become an at-home mom. Once she had two kids, Jane realized she was missing too much. "I felt my kids needed more attention. I was envious of my friends who were staying home."

Instead of searching for another daycare, she and her husband quickly figured that they could make it on a smaller income if they didn't need to pay for daycare and other work-related expenses. Jane seized an opportunity to shift into a lower-rung job at the bank with flexible evening and weekend hours and the same benefits.

Jane says now that she's home, it's easier to give her son the special attention he needs to be academically ready for school. She's grateful for the time to play with her kids and keep them busy—and away from the TV.

Her husband, Jim, an accountant, works about fifty hours a week during regular business hours and cares for the kids while Jane works two weekday evenings and Saturdays.

Because of Jim's careful bookkeeping at home, the family has had to make only small sacrifices to live on one-and-a-half incomes. For example, they vacation in Dubuque, Iowa, instead of at Disney World. "It's a cheaper vacation," Jane says, "and the kids have a lot of fun with their cousins." Jane is careful to avoid spending money during the day. "I know how to do a hundred and one free things in the city," she says. "We go to the zoo, the aquarium, go swimming. You've got to keep them busy, but you don't have to spend a lot of money to have fun."

"Staying home is much harder than you can ever imagine," she concludes, "but it's so rewarding. Some people think only people with money can stay home with their kids. That's not true. It costs money to go to work every day. There are alternatives."

Quality Parenting Is Job One

Brian, a former marketing project manager, and his wife, Susie, a software engineer, always knew one of them would stay home when they had children. "We discussed staying home even before Susie was pregnant," Brian explains, "and made a final decision during the pregnancy. We both understood that one of us should stay home. By default, I did, because she earned more and had more earning potential. Also, it interested me to be a stay-at-home parent." They both valued the security and safety they had experienced growing up in families with a parent at home. And they questioned their friends' and coworkers' attitude that daycare was a given.

They crunched the numbers just to make sure it would work. They determined that by eliminating daycare and other work-related expenses like commuting and dry cleaning costs, they could live on Susie's income. To stay within budget, they had to be more deliberate about big-ticket purchases. For example, they delayed buying a new computer a couple of years longer than they'd have liked and they recently bought a used mini-van instead of a new one.

When each of their two children was born, Susie took a twelve-week parental leave. (See pages 26–27 for more information on the Family and Medical Leave Act of 1993.) When her leaves ended, she continued to breastfeed by pumping at work. Brian has attended Early Childhood Family Education, a program funded by their Minnesota school district, where he's met other parents—mostly moms—and learned a lot about his new responsibilities.

Life as an at-home dad of a two-year-old and an infant is "a little mundane on a day-to-day basis," Brian admits. "But I geared myself up for the role. If you went to a job and your boss asked you to make copies, would you say no? You have to immerse yourself in *all* aspects of the job and get the job done. If I do that consistently—stick with that thought process—it helps me avoid the potential ruts. In the big picture, I group all these days into years. The goal is: They'll turn out to be good kids and they'll appreciate what we've done."

The At-Home Parent in North America

Throughout History

Deciding how to integrate child rearing with income-producing work may seem to be a modern-day issue, but it's actually as old as humankind. People have always struggled to balance the work of reproduction (bearing and raising children) with the work of production (acquiring food and shelter and participating in the community's economic life). In the beginning, this struggle was mainly about survival—gathering enough nuts and berries to keep everyone alive and finding a safe place to spend the night.

But through the millenia, many civilizations have evolved away from survival mode. In North America, for example, most people are no longer concerned solely about making it through the day, or the cold season, or the drought. We've devised complex systems of material and cultural value, and most of us have the luxury to choose where and how we'll live. As a result, our attitudes toward both kinds of work have changed.[1]

The role of parents shifted as nomadic societies became settled farming communities. Towns developed, and people began specializing in trades. Parents reared their children at home, most mothers nursed their babies, and the average household produced its own food, clothing, and tools.

The industrial revolution did not bode well for women and children. During the eighteenth and nineteenth centuries, Western economies became reliant on machinery rather than tools, and laborers—who'd formerly worked mainly on farms—were drawn to factories in cities. Factory workers were more dependent on their employers than rural workers had been. People in positions of power began to see children and adults of the working classes in terms of their economic—not human—value. As a result, the industrial machine shredded many working-class family systems. Meanwhile, the upper classes put women on pedestals in quicksand: Motherhood was upheld as sacred and important, but it was also undermined by women's restricted or nonexistent rights to own property, vote, and work—in short, to participate in public and economic life.

The industrial model of economy is still chugging along in the Western world. Though technology and civil rights have improved, families still face many of the same challenges their forebears did as they try to balance child rearing with income-producing work. For more than half of the twentieth century, staying home to care for the kids was the mom's job—at least in middle-class white North America. The norm for women in this segment of society was to work before the kids came along, but to stay home afterward, never to worry about earning a living again unless they were unlucky enough to become widowed or—*shhh!*—divorced.

Feminists throughout our nation's history, most recently those who raised our consciousness in the 1960s and 1970s (again, mostly white, middle-class women), have bravely and persistently offered a different vision of womanhood: one that is self-determined rather than role- or rule-based. They've helped women by opening doors to careers once reserved for their husbands and brothers and fathers and by elevating women's contributions and perspectives in all areas of life. They achieved this, however, partly by separating motherhood from womanhood. The question of who raises our children has, perhaps, seemed less compelling than the question of who runs our corporations, administers our universities, writes our laws, flies our airplanes, directs our films, and edits our newspapers.

The Working-Class Perspective

Many women in other segments of North American society haven't had the luxury of philosophizing about motherhood, nor have they needed to strong-arm their way out of the house and into the wage-earning world. Working-class American women have always done both kinds of work.

African-American women, for example, have a long history of such job juggling. During slavery, of course, they were forced to work outside the home. Their maternal rights were completely denied, and their work as domestics or field laborers was unpaid. When slavery ended, the options available to most African-American women didn't expand much. Their families needed the income they could now earn as much as their presence at home, and their value as workers hinged largely on their domestic and field skills. Furthermore, southern white society expected them to work and continued to depend on their labor. In the words of a former slave who migrated north after the Civil War, black women in Mississippi "were never allowed to stay at home as long as they were able to go. Had to take whatever they paid you for your work."

Even outside the South and well into the twentieth century, most African-American women kept working because they had to. They were either supporting themselves or making necessary contributions to their families' incomes. Census data from 1900 to 1920 reveal that while white women tended to drop out of the work force in their early twenties, black women often stayed in it through middle age.[2] This pattern continued throughout the twentieth century. In 1940, almost 40 percent of black middle-class wives worked outside the home, compared with 17 percent of white middle-class wives. By 1970, those numbers increased to 70 percent versus 45 percent, and by 1994, the figures had climbed to 87 percent versus 78 percent.

This long history in the work force often puts contemporary African-American parents who want to stay home with their kids in a sticky situation: Their families and culture place a high value on their ability to contribute financially and achieve professionally, so those who choose to stay home may find they must constantly justify their decision.[3]

In my own travels, I frequently see immigrant women of various nationalities and ethnicities working jobs that many middle-class white women don't want. They cook and clean and do laundry and care for others' children in others' homes. They scrub bathrooms and floors in airports and motel rooms and office buildings. They sew clothes in factories and take fees in parking lots. Sometimes they work in family businesses—Asian groceries and restaurants come to mind. Then these women go home to raise their children and do their families' domestic work. They do not enjoy the luxury of choice. They work outside the home—as many of our ancestors did—to make a better life for their children and their children's children.

Those of us who have benefited from such material sacrifices—as well as from the efforts of feminists who have fought to create a culture in which all parents have rights and choices—do well to consider our options with care. When we do so, our predecessors' work bears fruit.

Who's Making the Choice Today?

Rising housing costs, expensive medical insurance premiums, saving for college tuition and retirement…. The cost of living seems astronomical these days, and many families need all the income they can get. Choosing to be a stay-at-home parent may seem to be the privilege of those with six-figure incomes. Yet according to the U.S. Census Bureau, 43 percent of all adults ages 25–44 (and 72 percent of women ages 25–44) who do not participate in the paid work force say it is because they are taking care of children or others.[4]

To Stay or Not to Stay?

Choosing whether to stay home with your child is a complex task. To make the right choice, you must weigh the pros and cons of stay-at-home parenting in the context of your own family. First, let's look at the cons.

Some Reasons Parents Don't Stay Home

There are several good reasons why both parents may decide to keep working full-time outside the home:

- They determine that their family won't be able to survive on one income.

- They want to protect their careers. Women, especially, are in danger of being relegated to the "mommy track" and permanently losing professional ground.

- They fear for their mental health for any number of reasons, including the inevitable isolation and boredom of being home all day with a child as well as the loss of self-esteem and professional identity that may result from quitting a job.

- They struggle with the gender issues surrounding at-home parenthood. Women, for example, may feel that they're abandoning their feminist values to stay home. Men may feel insecure about joining the small minority of at-home dads.

- They place a high value on the creative and social rewards of work.

- They believe that they'll be very unhappy as at-home parents and that their child will suffer as a result.

Census Shows More At-Home Moms of Infants

An October 2001 report from the U.S. Census Bureau states: "From 1998 to 2000, the overall labor force participation rate of mothers with infants dropped from 59 percent to 55 percent." This decline was most significant among a relatively small group of parents: married, white women over thirty with some college education. I certainly can't say if this marks the beginning of a long-term swing toward more parents choosing to stay home, but it may indicate that when parents *can* choose to be home, they prefer to do so.

Source: Amara Bachu and Martin O'Connell, *Fertility of American Women: June 2000,* Current Population Reports, U.S. Census Bureau, Washington, DC (2001).

- They worry that their retirement savings won't cover their needs if they drop out of the paid work force, even temporarily.

- They face health insurance obstacles. For example, the higher-paid spouse may not have employer-subsidized health insurance.

- They feel that their child's social development and communication skills will benefit from regular interaction with other children and caring adults.

What's Best for Mom Is Best for the Family

Jo is a mother of two in Columbus, Ohio. Penny is raising four children in Lander, Wyoming. Each considered staying home to parent but in the end chose to return to her job. Their stories are similar: While at home with their babies, they craved the stimulation of contact with adults outside the family. Neither had a strong support network of friends and family nearby while her children were infants. Both found trustworthy daycare and flexible employment. Under these circumstances, these women are happiest balancing employment and parenting. Penny says, "I have a friend from back home in North Carolina who has four kids and chose to home-school. That is so not me!" But she respects her friend's decision because that's what makes her friend happy. In the end, she says, "The woman should do what's best for her, because what's best for her is ultimately best for her family. If she's frustrated, where does she take it out?"

This Mom Is No Lone Ranger

When Jo's first-born arrived five years ago, Jo took a three-month parental leave, unsure about returning to work as a nurse practitioner and nursing teacher at a large state university. "I had no idea how I'd feel when the baby was born," Jo said. To maintain her professional credentials, Jo must practice a certain number of hours and recertify every five years. She never intended to stay home for good, but she didn't think taking a few years off would jeopardize her career. Money was not a factor in Jo's decision; she and her husband Steve, an environmental engineer, were comfortable living on one income.

But Jo soon discovered that she felt isolated being alone with an infant all day. "After Erin was born was the loneliest time in my life," she recalls. "I was the Lone Ranger with my shirt off, breastfeeding constantly!" Few other families in her funky urban neighborhood had young children, and her friends were either childless or parents of teenagers. The slow rhythm of life with a baby didn't suit her personality well. "When I was on maternity leave, my house was never cleaner! I felt like I had to be doing something all the time."

Jo decided to go back to the teaching half of her job and gradually ramped up to full-time by resuming clinical work. She has since earned a second master's degree and given birth to her second child. Her kids, she says, are in "the world's greatest daycare," and that gives her confidence in her choice. It's available only to university employees, staffed by childhood development specialists and student interns, and so close to her office that she walked over to breastfeed her son several times a day until he started taking a bottle.

From Financial Need to Emotional Fulfillment

Penny was the primary wage earner in her family. Her husband, John, was a graduate student in mathematics earning a small teaching assistant's wage. So when their first child was born, she "planned all along to go back to work." A close friend who was an at-home mother cared for the baby while Penny held an office job she liked in Madison, Wisconsin.

But by the time Penny's second child was born eighteen months later, the family had moved to Lander, Wyoming, far from friends and family. Penny and John decided she would stay home with the kids while he taught high school math. But Penny, a journalism and political science major in college, realized quickly that being at home with an infant and a toddler was not for her. It was a difficult winter in small-town Wyoming, with little opportunity for social contact with other parents of young children or for intellectual stimulation through community involvement.

"I found I didn't have the patience to be a full-time stay-at-home mom," Penny says. "Marshall was born in September; I lasted until April!" When the couple decided one of them needed to work the following summer because John was on a nine-month school contract, Penny jumped at the chance to get out of the house. She landed an office job at a nationally known outdoor education school. There, she says, "I met lots of like-minded people, which was really what I needed—a way to get out and have adult conversation."

Penny has since returned to school to become a nurse. She now works at a dialysis clinic, which offers the flexible schedule she needs to balance the logistics of life with four children ranging in age from pre-school to junior high. While the struggle to balance school, work, and family life leaves little time for herself, Penny knows it's the mix that works best for her right now—and that means it works best for her family as a whole.

If you're struggling with any of the concerns described above, know that you're in good company. And whatever parenting arrangement you eventually choose, rest secure in the knowledge that you have weighed your options carefully and have followed the path you believe is best for your family.

Now, let's look at the upside of at-home parenting.

Some Reasons Parents Choose to Stay Home

Many parents stay home with their children because:

- They want to be with their children.
- They want to enhance the physical and psychological well-being of their families with a calm, stable, continuous parental presence at home.

- They want to make sure their children receive the first fruits of their energy and wisdom.

- They want to avoid the stress of juggling job responsibilities and family responsibilities.

- They question the quality of daycare options available to them.

- They want to make it easier to nurse their babies.

- They want to guide their school-age children or teens as they watch their children grow and change and become influenced by peers or values they absorb at school or elsewhere.

- They reject the gender stereotypes associated with work and parenting. For example, a mother who works outside the home may seek release from the expectation that she must "do it all." A father may disagree with the notion that he should be the breadwinner, not the bread baker.

- They didn't know how strongly they would feel about being with their children until they became parents.

- They could successfully balance employment and child care with one child, but upon having a second, they find that the rewards of employment are not worth the cost of having two kids in daycare and/or the stress it puts on the family routine.

The emotional benefits you reap if you or your partner decides to stay home may well outweigh the financial, professional, and other costs. For example, most families with an at-home parent never worry about whether their child is being cared for in a loving, safe, and appropriate environment. Many women who stay home eliminate the unmerited but oft-reported guilt induced by the demands of workplace and family, as well as the stress of doing two full-time jobs: parenting/household management and paid employment.

Simply being with your child offers many rewards, too. By staying home, you can share as much of your child's journey as possible, building competence and confidence as a parent every step of the way. You can see your child's world through his or her eyes in all its detail and freshness.

"Now I know what I could miss," said Jeanne, who directed a human services planning agency before leaving her job to be home with her toddler and infant. "Had I never known it, I would have been okay, and they would have been, too. But I'm really happy to be here." The big and small moments that make memories—the funny expressions, the irresistible face covered with ice cream, the discovery of a spider web or a bright red cardinal—happen when they happen, not necessarily when parents squeeze "quality time" with their kids into a busy day.

Finally, there's no getting around the fact that you love your child more than any substitute caregiver could. Choosing to give your child and yourself the gift of sustained time together is a way to honor the life you share. It's also a great way to give your child the routine, stability, and security that's so important to his or her overall development.

Deciding Who Stays Home

Thank goodness we've evolved beyond the model of the TV-rerun family, in which a mother in pearls and perfectly coiffed hair is the director of all things domestic. Now many two-parent families are exploring alternatives to the full-time stay-at-home mom. Dads are staying home in some families, especially when mom earns more money or has a more promising career. In other families, both parents work flexible schedules so that one parent is always—or almost always—at home.

Good Old Mom

Throughout human history, women's role in parenting has differed from men's simply because of biology: Women are the ones who are pregnant and who breastfeed their babies. This biological reality means that children bond with and need their mothers differently than they bond with and need their fathers. Gender roles in the family and society developed at least in part from this biological reality.

Even today, the need to breastfeed dictates that many women stay near their offspring. Mothers want to give their babies the best start in life, and according to widespread medical consensus, that includes breastfeeding. Pediatricians recommend it for an infant's first year.[5] Breastfeeding is much simpler when done at home and on a baby's schedule rather than between meetings and phone calls behind a locked office door. Families who have more than one child may experience a childbearing "burst" during which the mother alternates between pregnancy and breastfeeding for a few to several years. During these years devoted to the great physical demands of reproduction, life may be simpler and saner—not to mention less sleep-deprived—if mom is at home.

However, thanks to changing gender roles and attitudes about caregiving, increasingly flexible employment policies, and technological advances like breast pumps and baby formula that allow babies to meet their nutritional needs without mothers at hand, men can do the work moms have done for millennia—and do it well.

The Dad Advantage

A growing number of families count dads as their children's primary caregivers. In 1996, 18 percent of all children ages zero to five in the United States had their fathers as primary caregivers while their mothers were working outside the home, attending school, or looking for work.[6] But despite some recent studies on stay-at-home dads, it's difficult to come up with an exact percentage, says Robert Frank, a Chicago psychologist who has researched at-home dads. That's because the response to the question *Who is the child's primary caregiver?* depends on how you define *primary caregiver*. In his research, Frank counted as the primary caregiver the

Quantity Time

Research shows that the average amount of time children actually spend with their parents is very low, and the time they spend in conversation with them is even lower. "Real Vision," a project of the TV-Turnoff Network, reports that children and parents spend an average of only 38.5 minutes per week in meaningful conversation, while children ages 2–17 spend an average of 19 hours and 40 minutes per week watching TV. A recent study by Ellen Galinsky of the Work Family Institute found that 28 percent of dual-earner parents said that they play or exercise with their children every day, while only 6 percent of kids agreed that this is the case. And 36 percent of dual-earner parents said they do homework with their kids "five or six times a week" or "every day," while only 19 percent of kids concurred.

Sources: Tony Schwartz, "Life/Work – Issue 31," in *Fast Company Online*, http://pf.fastcompany.com/online/31/tschwartz.html (accessed March 6, 2002).

"Facts and Figures about Our TV Habit," TV-Turnoff Network.

Wired for Sound

Some research shows that men and women experience equivalent instinctual responses to the sound of a baby in intense distress (such as the cry of a baby being circumcised), though women respond more consistently and quickly to lesser cries of discomfort. Anthropologists suggest that the nursing bond and the probability that a mom's "lower threshold for responding to infant signals is innate" reinforce behaviors that encourage many moms to accept a primary caregiving role.

Source: Sarah Blaffer Hrdy, *Mother Nature*, p. 212.

adult who spent at least thirty hours per week with the youngest child; that person had to be there more than any other adult.[7] Kristin Smith, a researcher with the U.S. Census Bureau, agrees with Frank that how the question is asked is important. She notes, for example, that a father may be at home full-time while he is unemployed and looking for work, but he intends to return to the labor force as soon as possible and thus doesn't consider himself the primary caregiver. At-home fatherhood is a hot topic; Smith says that the Census Bureau expects to publish a report on stay-at-home dads in 2004.[8]

Dads may have an advantage in bringing less emotional baggage to stay-at-home parenting than women often do. It's not that at-home dads don't struggle with some of the same issues moms do—and certainly, as a minority among stay-at-home parents, they have their own problems with identity and isolation. Consider, for example, how stressful it might be to buck the age-old societal expectation that men provide for their families' material needs. However, my guess is that they're wired differently in terms of their emotional responses to the work of child care—perhaps more inclined to take care of their own needs and less weighted by parenting "shoulds" than moms tend to be.

For example, despite their feminist enlightenment, many women I know still struggle with perfectionist tendencies toward keeping their houses tidy and their children in matching socks. More than a few dads, on the other hand, have been known to overlook the dirty details when they're on kid duty. Case in point: A mom of six reports that when her husband took several of the kids to the family's vacation cabin for a long weekend, the children returned home in the same T-shirts they'd been wearing when they left, now embellished with food stains and dirt— testimony to their wonderful, worry-free time with dad. And once I returned from a solo trip to find a half-full cup of coffee I'd hastily left on the bathroom shelf still sitting there. My husband and three kids were happy and healthy, I'm glad to report, and they may even have been clad in clean T-shirts.

Of course, many dads balance children and chores gracefully. Dave, a dad of two teens, accepts that his role as at-home parent includes the cleaning. He says it's only rational: "If [my wife's] going to work long hours to bring in money, I have the responsibility to use my time productively at home." Besides, he adds, "I'm in the house so many hours a day, I want it to be a pleasant place."

Though it's increasingly common to see a dad at midday in the park or the grocery store or the doctor's office with his children, some dads still get asked if they're baby-sitting or get funny looks from neighborhood busybodies. One at-home dad laughed as he described how some men on his block wondered if they should be worried about their wives spending so much time with him. But here's the good news: A child whose father is the primary caregiver may have better relationships with both parents than a child whose mom stays home while dad works. According to Dr. Frank's studies, in families with mom bringing home the bacon and dad frying it up, the children are equally likely to go to either parent if they wake up during the middle of the night. In "traditional" families, 80 percent of children awakened during the night go to mom first.[9]

Tag-Team Parenting

Another growing trend among families is for mom and dad to share child-care responsibilities by staggering their work schedules and taking turns at home. Tag-team parents reap some benefits that single-earner families miss:

- Both parents continue to earn income, which may reduce the financial strain of at-home parenting.

Share-Care Families Embody Cultural Trend

In an interview with Keith H. Hammonds in the magazine *Fast Company Online,* social analyst Helen Wilkinson says that men's willingness to share domestic roles and the business world's recognition of the value of traditionally feminine skills like communications and conflict resolution signify that the boundaries between male and female roles at home, at work, and in society are changing for the better. In fact, Wilkinson says, we are entering an "age of androgyny." Not that we'll all be wearing unisex clothes and haircuts—rather, she says, our cultural choices will increasingly rely on a "convergence between family relationships and paid work."

Wilkinson cautions, however, that although corporate and government policies, such as the Family and Medical Leave Act of 1993, have begun to address this social reality, they have not kept pace—and that children bear the costs of this tentative progress. Therefore, families must continue to forge their own paths to suit their particular circumstances.

Source: Keith H. Hammonds, "Work and Life–Helen Wilkinson," *Fast Company Online,* 30, (December 1999): 188.

- Both parents continue to reap the social, intellectual, and professional rewards of working outside the home.

- Both parents are directly involved in their child's life.

On the downside, some tag-team parents still have to deal with daycare. For example, each parent may put in a condensed, three- or four-day workweek to provide two to four days of at-home parenting. This arrangement produces many of the benefits of stay-at-home parenting and reduces the need for daycare—but doesn't eliminate it. And most tag-team parents must work harder to make time for each other and for the entire family to be together.

In one family, parents Doug and Marian decided to share the care of their children while both continued to work. (Doug is a school social worker, and Marian works in mortgage sales.) It wasn't so much about finances for them, but about values. It was important to both of them to maintain their career skills *and* keep their children primarily in a parent's care until they were old enough to attend school. For eight years, Marian spent her days with the kids and worked evenings until eleven o'clock or later. Doug and Marian often had only ten minutes of handoff time to exchange quick information about the children and household after he arrived home from work and before she left for her job. They preserved weekends for family time, and they also enjoyed summers and school holidays when Doug was home.

Making the Right Choice for Your Family

Deciding whether to stay home and who should stay home is both an emotional and a financial cost-benefit analysis. There's no single solution to this puzzle; each family must make a decision within the context of its own particular needs and circumstances. To start your analysis off right, let's take a closer look at the five main factors that affect parents' decisions about staying home:

- Income
- Career
- Gender
- Personality
- Daycare

As you read about these issues, consider how they play out in your family.

The Big Five

Living on Less

It's hard to choose deliberately to earn less money. Some families are already stretched to the maximum on two incomes. Choosing less also seems to ignore the reality of the rising cost of living in many parts of the country. Finally, it goes against the grain of North American culture. Our society tends to focus on the validation power of a hefty paycheck, an impressive job title, a nice office, an annual raise, and other workplace measures of worth. It's telling that we pay child-care workers poorly and don't even count domestic work in our gross national product.

We must measure the value of staying home by a different system than the one our marketplace reflects. The nurturing of each precious child is a huge, important undertaking requiring knowledge and skills in psychology, communications, human development, management, and organization. Staying home with children is not for wimps or those who lack ambition; it's for people with determination, grit, creativity, and the courage to make hard choices like reducing family income.

If you're concerned about the financial impact of at-home parenting on your family, see Chapter 2: Money Matters for financial planning advice, money-saving tips, an in-depth look at the costs of working outside the home, and ideas for generating income at home.

Chutes and (Career) Ladders

If money matters occupy the fronts of most people's minds as they consider stay-at-home parenting, the back story is the emotional struggle parents often experience as they leave the paid work force. Staying home may be a big sacrifice for those who've invested lots of time and money in education and paying their dues. Many people really love what they do, whether they're in Silicon Valley, on Wall Street, in the Ivy League, onstage, on-line, or on call. It can be hard to imagine leaving it all behind.

Postponing career advancement is another reason some parents can't see quitting their jobs. Parents report that coworkers and customers may assume their commitment to work is diminished if the parent attempts to arrange part-time work or a flexible schedule in order to accommodate family responsibilities.

I've experienced this firsthand. After my third child was born, I negotiated a job share that cut my hours at a social service agency from three days a week to just one. One day a coworker commented, "Must be nice to work part-time." Her tone implied that I was getting away with something! Sure, I was working fewer hours, but I was also earning less money and fewer benefits.

Another mother, who held a high-profile consulting job, describes "an undercurrent" of suspicion that she was "less than fully committed to the work" when she returned three days a week instead of full-time after a three-month parental leave following the birth of her first child.

A third, a partner at a law firm, lost points—the points by which partners were allocated compensation—because the other partners perceived her as less than "gung ho" about her work while she juggled the needs of her newborn and her dying mother. "The senior partner didn't like this at all," says this mom of two, who later left her job and now freelances from home investigating sexual harassment cases and employment issues.

And a mother of two-year-old twins, ready to go back to work full-time in the school district where she'd worked for nine years, lost her place on the promotion ladder after taking an extended leave of absence to stay home with her sons.

If you're upwardly mobile in your field, staying home to care for your child may keep you on a lower rung for a longer time than if you return to your job soon after the baby's born. But it doesn't mean you'll fall off the ladder entirely. Whether you decide to stay home for one year or several, there are ways to keep up with your career. You can maintain membership in professional associations, perhaps volunteering to serve on a committee; keep reading trade publications; and stay in touch with coworkers, customers, or others in your field. Laurie, a lawyer with three children, volunteers on a local government committee. She attends meetings for a few hours at a time once or twice a month, even though it can be a hassle to switch gears from her parenting work or negotiate child care to accommodate frequent last-minute schedule changes. "It's a way to keep my finger in the pie," she says.

For more ideas on how to stay connected in your field, turn your at-home experience into an employment asset, and reenter the job market, see Chapter 6: Everything Changes.

Bending Gender Expectations

As we discussed on page 19, North American culture tends to measure success in numbers and status symbols. It also values making a difference in the world through one's own creative efforts and hard work. Many women believe that as feminists in America, their place is out in the world, breaking the glass ceiling, earning money, competing in the marketplace, making a difference through their creativity, intelligence, expertise, and skills.

But I think feminism is really about women having choices. A woman's place, then, is where she wants to be—and for many women, at least for part of their lives, that's at home with their children.

If you're a woman who chooses to stay home with her child, you're not negating years of hard-won advances toward a woman-friendly world. Most at-home moms aren't interested in living a vision of idealized housewifely bliss—becoming a June Cleaver or Carol Brady whose identity revolves around her roles as wife, mother, and homemaker. That vision is a Madison Avenue fallacy anyway, as Betty Friedan explained decades ago in her classic book *The Feminine Mystique*. Staying

Ditto for Dads

Men, too, can suffer professionally from putting their families first. Todd was working as a title examiner when his first child was born. When he returned from a mere four days off, his boss scolded him for shirking his "responsibilities" to care for his wife, who was having a difficult recovery from childbirth. (Todd is now self-employed.) And Darcy reports that when her husband, Bruce, missed four weeks of work going to Russia to adopt their daughter, "his pay was cut and his job threatened just for this partial leave."

home with your children is not a denial of the you that existed before motherhood and continues to exist—the productive, creative, ambitious, income-producing, market-validated you. As at-home mother of three and independent radio producer Nanci Olesen says, "My feminism is well in place. If anything, I feel defensive toward those who think it's not possible to be domestic and productive *and* equal. I would say, look again."

Women who stay home with children can nurture their "productive and equal" selves by choosing to make time for their passions through community involvement, creative pursuits, or volunteer leadership. In fact, some women find that parenting enhances their political awareness and commitment to building systems that help all women and children. For example, Olesen produces a radio show about mothers that began as a volunteer project for a community radio station. She's also the chair of the board of directors at her children's school. Another mom, Jeanne, is passionate about her service on a neighborhood board currently wrestling with major transportation issues. She contributes to her community and sets an example of participative democracy for her children.

Discussing household division of labor is another way to buck gender bias in family life. Remember that forging nontraditional roles and identities is more than dads doing dishes and moms mowing lawns. Successful at-home parenting depends on both partners buying into the importance of having a parent at home and making choices that allow the at-home partner to get social, creative, intellectual, emotional, and physical needs met on a regular basis. Maggie, a former at-home mom of two, says, "It's important for partners [who aren't at home] to experience being home with the kids by themselves so they can really, truly be supportive."

Women aren't the only parents who wrestle with gender issues as they consider staying home. Brian, at home with his infant and preschool-age daughters, says he doesn't miss his old marketing job too much. "I have some inner struggles, but nothing overwhelming," he says. Still, some days he ponders what his peers are doing: "I go out for a walk and see other guys on telephone poles, driving buses, in their cars, and I think, 'What are they doing today?' Or I wonder, 'What do they think of me?'" But Brian knows he's not alone. "Last summer I ran into a musician [dad] who works at night and stays home during the day. You realize other people are doing it. Women we hang out with—that helps, too. They're making the same choices and sacrifices."

Am I Cut Out for This?

"What on earth will I do with a baby all day?" you might ask. Perhaps you question your abilities as caregiver and teacher. (If so, check out Chapter 3: Caring for Your Child for basic information on nutrition, sleep, discipline, fun, and learning.)

Or maybe you're wondering if you'll be happy on the home front. It's true: Hanging out with a young child for hours on end

Intangible Rewards

In her book *The Time Bind*, sociologist Arlie Hochschild reveals the results of her study of how a range of employees at a midsize American corporation balanced home and work. Sometimes company policies made the balancing act difficult. But in other cases, work became a refuge for parents who struggled with the constant needs of their families.

Hochschild's study offers evidence that both men and women in blue-collar, pink-collar, and white-collar jobs often believe they get something out of their work that they don't get at home—such as camaraderie with coworkers, the reward of feeling productive, and time to themselves away from the demands of family members. (Sure, employers make demands, but they don't usually do so while banging on the bathroom door.)

It's All Relative

I have a friend who works part-time as a freelance assistant TV director. Her husband is in the same business, and sometimes their on-location assignments overlap. For these situations, her three boys have a "nanny"—their aunt, who happens to be a registered nurse and a parent herself. That, without a doubt, is as good as it gets.

But even what seems like the ideal daycare situation—grandma's house—can be hard to handle when conflicts arise. Jane, a mother of two, paid her mother-in-law eight hundred dollars a month to care for her children while she worked full-time as a personal banker. But when Jane grew dissatisfied with the lack of structure and amount of TV her kids watched at grandma's, she found it hard to call it quits because of their family relationship. Eventually grandma announced she'd be caring for a new infant in the family and could no longer care for Jane's children—just the reason Jane needed to switch to part-time work so she could be home during the days.

could try the patience of Mr. Rogers. Children love repetition. They're messy. They don't usually climb into their car seats and buckle themselves in, requesting National Public Radio as you go about your errands. They're prone to questioning everything. There's no sure cure for the feeling that you simply cannot stand to play go fish or hide-and-seek for the seventeenth time. One woman with typically curious, walking and climbing fifteen-month-old twins remarked, "I have days when I just lie on the floor and think, 'I have to get myself up to get an iced coffee.'" Times like this are when remembering the big picture—trusting your instinct that you're doing the right thing for your kids—is the only way to cope. Or when little things like iced coffee, calling a friend, or a longer-than-usual nap can make your day. It also helps to keep in mind that today, staying home with children is usually a fluid situation—parents at home are seldom home forever. (For more information about staying sane on the home front and adapting to changing family circumstances, see Chapter 4: Caring for You and Chapter 6: Everything Changes.)

The Daycare Dilemma

For many parents, deciding whether to stay home is linked to their comfort level with using nonparental child care. This comfort level, in turn, often depends on the quality, cost, and types of care available. Parents' primary choices are daycare centers, often operated as franchises or through non-profit organizations like houses of worship; licensed home daycare, where children are cared for by providers in their homes; unlicensed home daycare—often less expensive but not regulated or evaluated by licensing officials; and nannies or baby sitters who care for children in the children's homes. Licensed facilities may be regulated according to health and safety standards, ratio of caregivers to children, and staff training requirements. Nannies and baby sitters may be screened by agencies or by the families who hire them.

Many parents want to believe our society's message that daycare is okay for kids. And it's true that children can thrive in daycare as well as in the care of their parents. Numerous studies have shown that high-quality daycare is associated with enhanced social skills, reduced behavior problems, increased cooperation, and improved language in children.[10] But as parents begin searching for child care, they often realize that the available and affordable options aren't necessarily desirable ones.

Unfortunately, research suggests that the quality of child care in the United States is generally mediocre.[11] That's not surprising, given how poorly we pay child-care workers. According to the Occupational Employment Statistics survey conducted in 2000 by the U.S. Bureau of Labor Statistics, child-care workers and preschool teachers earn average hourly wages of $7.86 and $9.66, respectively. Only eighteen occupations out of the seven hundred surveyed pay less. Service station attendants, tree trimmers, bicycle repairers, and crossing guards all earn more.[12]

Evaluating Your Child-Care Options

Child Care Aware is a national nonprofit organization that connects parents with child-care resources in their communities and educates parents on how to choose high-quality care. To tap this pipeline of valuable, easy-to-use information, call 800-424-2246 or visit http://www.childcareaware.org.

Daycare Sticker Shock

Despite the dismal earnings of U.S. child-care workers, daycare is one of the biggest budget items in many households—right up there with housing, health insurance, and groceries. Care for a four-year-old at child-care centers around the country costs an average of four to six thousand dollars per year. This is more than the average yearly tuition at most public colleges and universities.

Source: Karen Schulman, "The High Cost of Child Care Puts Quality Care Out of Reach for Many Families," Children's Defense Fund, Washington, DC (2000).

FMLA Basics

Here's a primer on the Family and Medical Leave Act. For more information, contact the nearest office of the Wage and Hour Division, listed in most directories under "U.S. Government, Department of Labor." Or hop on-line and visit http://www.dol.gov/esa/whd/fmla/.

An employee is eligible if all of these conditions are met:

- The employer has fifty or more employees who work within a seventy-five-mile radius.
- The employee has worked for the employer for at least one year.
- The employee has worked at least 1,250 hours over the previous twelve months.

An employee is entitled to twelve weeks of unpaid leave during any twelve-month period for any of these reasons:

- To care for the employee's child after birth, adoption, or placement for foster care.
- To care for the employee's spouse, child, or parent who has a serious health condition.
- For a serious health condition that makes the employee unable to perform his or her job.

By so poorly compensating the people who care for our nation's children, our marketplace value system implies that child care is not challenging or important work and that almost anyone can do it. Child-care workers, who know that their efforts are undervalued, respond with a turnover rate of 30 to 40 percent a year.[13]

The bottom line is that parents must look closely at both the cost and the quality of care available for their children. Once your child bonds with a caregiver and gets used to a routine, it's hard to change even if you discover you're not happy with the situation.

The Family and Medical Leave Act of 1993

Our society is beginning to recognize that balancing family life and work life is important. Because we no longer expect a worker to stay with the same employer for life, and because technology has radically changed how, when, and where we can work, parents now have more options for scheduling work and family time. And thanks to the Family and Medical Leave Act of 1993 (FMLA), many parents can stay home for at least a short time when they have a new child without losing ground at work.

The FMLA requires certain employers to grant an eligible employee a twelve-week unpaid leave upon the birth or adoption of a child and to restore the employee to the same or an equivalent job at the end of the leave. (Some highly paid employees are exempt from this guarantee.) If the parents in a two-parent family take twelve-week leaves consecutively, their newborn could spend the first six months of life in parental care.

Fighting for Your Rights in the Real World

Although FMLA is the law, not all employers go out of their way to inform their employees of their rights. Paul, who took a twelve-week leave under FMLA when his child was born, said his employer was initially "reluctant" about his request for leave, but in the end "very supportive." After Paul paved the way, other fathers at his company also took advantage of their rights.

During his leave, Paul went with his baby daughter to a drywall supply store and found himself in conversation with a clerk, who said that he would soon be a father, too. Paul encouraged him to look into his rights under FMLA while the store's manager stood behind the clerk, shaking his head as if to say, "Stop! Don't tell him!" Paul, undeterred, reminded the manager: "It's federal law."

A Checklist of Questions about Staying Home

It should be obvious that I think stay-at-home parenting is a great choice. But I also know it's a complex choice—and it's not the right choice for everyone. In this chapter, I've tried to present the benefits and challenges of at-home parenting honestly to help you make an educated decision. If you and your partner are still undecided, ask yourselves these questions:

◗ *Can we devise a livable one-income budget to follow?* Think about whether this budget would be in effect indefinitely or for a specific period of time

An employee may be required to provide:

• Thirty days advance notice when the leave is foreseeable.

• Medical certification of a serious health condition, second or third opinions (at the employer's expense), or a "fitness for duty" report upon returning to work.

An employee is entitled to these protections:

• For the duration of the leave, the employer must maintain the employee's coverage under any group health plan.

• Upon returning from leave, most employees must be restored to their original or equivalent positions with equivalent pay, benefits, and other employment terms.

• The employer cannot revoke any benefit accrued by the employee before the start of his or her leave.

Source: U.S. Department of Labor, Employment Standards Administration, "Your Rights under the Family and Medical Leave Act of 1993," WH Publication 1420 (June 1993).

●●●●●●●●●●●●●●●●●●●●

Beyond FMLA

If you're not eligible for FMLA leave, be sure to investigate your state's laws and your employer's policy, which may be different. If you're eligible for family leave under both federal and state laws, you're entitled to the greater benefit. If you're an adoptive parent, check out the following program:

Adoption and the Workplace

Address:
1500 Walnut Street, Suite 701
Philadelphia, Pennsylvania 19102

Phone:
800-TO-ADOPT (800-862-3678)

Fax:
215-735-9410

Email:
LBelcastro@nacenter.adopt.org

Web:
http://www.adopt.org/workplace

(for example, for a year or until your child is weaned, out of diapers, or ready to start school). Don't forget to look at how your tax status might change.

● *How important are our jobs to our identities and personal satisfaction?* Can one of you put your ambitions on the back burner indefinitely or for a specific time? Or negotiate a job share or an extended leave of absence?

● *Do we know the quality and cost of all our child-care options?*

● *Have we sought out stories from the trenches?* Career counselors advise informational interviews for people wanting to switch careers or land a dream job. Why not take advantage of the wisdom of folks who've walked in the shoes you'd like to try on? To get a balanced perspective, talk to both current and former stay-at-home moms and dads.

● *What are our values about child rearing?* Can you take the long-term view that by having a parent at home, you're making a sound investment in both your family's emotional capital as well as society's human capital?

No Simple Equation

There's no simple equation to determine conclusively whether staying home is right for you. Many parents—even those committed to their professions and happy in their work—find that their roles as mothers and fathers supersede everything else for at least a few years while their children are growing up. Despite the personal and professional costs, they choose to be their children's primary caregivers because they believe it's the best option for their kids. And despite the struggles, most say they would do it again.

Don't Ignore Your Instincts

It's amazing how many parents don't decide to stay home based on a completely rational look at the pros and cons. For many, including me, it's a gut-level choice. In retrospect there are many lesser choices I'd have made differently: I'd have been better informed and more deliberate about money and budgeting. I'd have felt much less conflicted about making time for myself. I'd have been more intentional about household organization. But given the chance, I would make the same big choice—to be a mom at home—in a heartbeat.

I'll leave the last word to a mother who worked at full tilt for more than a decade before deciding to quit her job and stay home. Her advice to parents in the midst of the choice: "Don't just make a pragmatic list of the pros and cons and financials and the nitty-gritty stuff. Ask yourself bigger questions, like what you're going to want your life to look like in retrospect. If you ask yourself those questions, you'll figure out how to make work whatever you want to work."

Chapter 2

Money Matters

Welcome to the home zone! If you've read past Chapter 1, you've probably decided to give at-home parenting a try. Congratulations on navigating that difficult decision—but be aware that you still have some challenging choices ahead.

There's no getting around it: Deciding to stay home with your child affects your family finances. It means you're intentionally reducing your income. If discussions about cold hard cash make you hot under the collar, you'd better chill out now. Like it or not, you and your partner need to honestly hash out your financial priorities and your feelings about the purpose of money. This is where the rubber meets the road for many families who want to have a parent at home. Even if you approach your task as a healthy challenge, as a character-building exercise, or as a romantic adventure, wrestling with the checkbook every week is sure to get old fast.

But the good news is that you don't have to be rich to choose at-home parenting. It's possible to live on one income—for a limited time or a lifetime—if you're honest and realistic, practice sound money management, communicate openly, and remember your priorities. This chapter will show you how.

Every Coin Has Two Sides

Public discussion about at-home parenting often revolves around the financial impact of the decision. And it's no wonder; raising a child is expensive. A family with a child born in 2001 can expect to spend the following on food, shelter, and other necessities to raise that child over the subsequent seventeen years:

- $169,920 for households with before-tax income under $39,100
- $231,470 for households with before-tax income of $39,100 to $65,800

◉ $337,690 for households with before-tax income above $65,800[1]

Advocates of staying home are quick to point out the costs of working—not only the obvious one, child care, but also such "hidden" expenses as the cost of commuting, a work wardrobe, dry cleaning, office celebrations, gifts, coffee breaks, and lunches out.

It's only fair to add that there are hidden costs in stay-at-home parenting, too. Stepping out of the work force to stay home with children means not only an immediate reduction in family income, but a long-term loss of resources. This loss is borne primarily by women, who wind up at the end of their lives with far less to live on than men because they've accrued smaller retirement savings and social security income than their husbands.

Let's look at both sides of the coin.

The Costs of Working

Middle-class couples who crunch the numbers while deciding whether to have one parent at home often find that their combined net yearly income, after subtracting daycare fees and other work-related expenses, is just a few thousand dollars more than they would net with one parent at home. How could that be? Add one big cost to a bunch of sneaky little ones, and—*poof*—a lot of money disappears.

The Bank Breaker: Child Care

Saving the cost of daycare is one huge incentive for parents to stay home. According to a report issued by the Children's Defense Fund (CDF), full-time care for an infant at an urban child-care center costs more per year than public college tuition in every U.S. state. The same is true for four-year-olds in every state except Vermont.[2]

The following table, which gives a sample of data from the CDF report, shows that child-care costs vary depending on location, type of care, and age of child. For example, child care is generally most expensive for infants, who need a lower children-to-caregiver ratio. Home-based child care usually costs less than care at licensed centers with more staff and overhead. And child care in rural areas tends to cost less than in cities. But even when these factors are considered, child care still often costs more than public college tuition.

Average Annual Child-Care Costs

STATE	URBAN AREAS Child-Care Center	Family Child Care	RURAL AREAS Child-Care Center	Family Child Care	PUBLIC COLLEGE TUITION
	Infant \ Preschooler	Infant \ Preschooler	Infant \ Preschooler	Infant \ Preschooler	
New Hampshire	$9,046 $6,520	$6,807 $6,058	$6,813 $5,595	$4,562 $4,374	$5,753
South Carolina	$4,004 $3,900	$3,640 $3,588	$3,380 $3,380	$3,120 $3,120	$3,520
Iowa	$6,750 $6,198	$4,950 $4,716	$5,278 $5,018	$4,248 $4,233	$2,869
Texas	$5,356 $4,160	$4,784 $4,160	$4,264 $3,068	$3,588 $3,276	$2,432
Colorado	$6,760 $5,096	$5,668 $5,200	$3,900 $3,380	$3,536 $3,536	$2,685
California	$6,995 $4,858	$5,533 $5,033	$7,188 $5,623	$4,993 $4,819	$2,609
Alaska	$7,176 $6,019	$6,450 $5,788	$7,475 $7,150	$7,475 $7,475	$2,769
Hawaii	$7,815 $5,505	$5,283 $5,113	$5,280 $4,846	$3,932 $3,907	$2,880

Source: Karen Schulman, "The High Cost of Child Care Puts Quality Care Out of Reach for Many Families," Children's Defense Fund, Washington, DC (2000).

Of course, the less a family earns, the higher the percentage of its income is eaten up by child care. Middle- and upper-income families typically spend 7 percent of their income on child care. But even if a low-income family managed to spend 10 percent of its income on child care, it would not be able to afford average-priced care—much less the steep prices charged by many high-quality providers.[3]

The Hole in Your Pocket: Other Work Expenses
If daycare is like a raid on the bank account, other work-related expenses are like an unnoticed hole in the pocket. Working outside the home often requires repeated small expenditures. Individually, these expenses are beneath notice. But tallied up over time, they can make a surprisingly large sum.

Transportation
This can be a major money-guzzler. Many families own two cars mainly because each parent needs one for traveling to and from work. Insurance, registration, gas, and maintenance costs for two vehicles add up to quite a chunk of change. If there are loan payments, parking fees, tolls, or traffic tickets in the equation, too, the chunk gets even bigger.

If one or both parents take public transportation to work, a family may still be forking over a lot of money for commuting. For example, a suburban Minneapolis resident who buses downtown five days a week can buy a "SuperSaver 31-Day Pass," which allows unlimited rides for a month (the transit authority's best deal for that situation). The pass costs eighty-five dollars a month—or over a thousand dollars per year.[4]

Working Wardrobe

Many workplaces have some kind of dress code. Depending on the job and the environment, expectations may range from "business casual" clothing (nice jeans or dress pants and shirts) to traditional business attire (suits) to uniforms. Workplace attire isn't usually the same type of clothing one wears on an ordinary day at home, so it must be counted as a job expense. Wardrobe costs may include purchasing clothing, shoes, accessories, and cosmetics; paying for dry cleaning; and getting more frequent (and possibly more expensive) haircuts or other treatments. One's professional image may include unexpected elements, too: A friend of mine, an architect and father of three, was actually chastised by his colleagues for driving an old minivan with some visible rust.

Food

Working outside the home often means spending more on meals and snacks. Harried parents may not have the time or energy to pack lunches for themselves or cook homemade meals all the time. As a result, they and their families may wind up eating costly convenience foods and/or restaurant meals more often.

2003 Federal Income Tax Rates for Married Individuals Filing Jointly

Taxable Income	Tax
$0–$12,000	10%
$12,001–$47,450	$1,200 + 15% of amount over $12,000
$47,451–$114,650	$6,517.50 + 27% of amount over $47,450
$114,651–$174,700	$24,661.50 + 30% of amount over $114,650
$174,701–$311,950	$41,676.50 + 35% of amount over $174,700
$311,951 and up	$90,714 + 38.6% of amount over $311,950

Source: CCH Tax Law Editors, *2003 U.S. Master Tax Guide*, CCH Incorporated (November 2002).

Taxes

In the United States, households that earn more money pay a higher percentage of their income to the federal government, and those that earn less pay a lower percentage. Consult an accountant to find out how much more income tax you pay as a dual-income household than you would with a single income. Or to get a general idea of the difference, check out the chart on the previous page.

Incidental Expenses

It's human nature to socialize, so most jobs involve some activities that are just for fun. These include things like football pools, group lottery ticket purchases, Girl Scout cookie sales, and collections for birthday, baby shower, wedding, and retirement gifts. These expenditures are voluntary, of course, but they're tempting because they offer employees pleasant diversions and ways to express their sense of community with each other.

Home Maintenance

Every home—from apartment to bungalow to mansion—requires maintenance to keep it livable. Parents who work outside the home sometimes find that they simply don't have the time or energy to maintain their homes to their liking, and many look for help. This might mean hiring someone to do weekly cleaning, enlisting professionals for repair or remodeling projects, or hiring baby sitters to care for the kids so parents can tackle household jobs themselves.

Job Maintenance

Finally, working outside the home may require spending on materials and information that help get the job done or help one stay competitive. Such expenditures include briefcases, personal computers, cell phones, personal digital assistants (PDAs), continuing education, licenses, association or union dues, subscriptions, club memberships, and any other career-related costs not reimbursed by employers.

The Costs of Staying Home

After reading about the costs of working, you might jump to the conclusion that stay-at-home parenting is the cheaper, simpler option. Not so fast! Staying home has its own financial costs—some you'll notice right away, some that could come back to haunt you.

In-Your-Face Income Reduction

This one's so obvious, it almost seems silly to mention it. But mention it we must, because it's the biggest financial challenge at-home parents face. In most cases, when parents rearrange their lives to accommodate at-home or tag-team parenting, they generate less income than they used to. Sometimes they lose an entire full-time salary when one parent quits his or her job. Sometimes the cut's less severe; for example, one or both parents may shift to a part-time schedule or take a lower-paying but more flexible job. But the hard truth is that there's usually less income to support the family.

Behind-Your-Back Income Reduction

In her book *The Price of Motherhood,* Ann Crittenden, a former *New York Times* reporter, estimates that she gave up about seven hundred thousand dollars when she quit her job to become a stay-at-home mom. This number may be shocking, but it's not inflated. According to economists, a college-educated American woman typically loses more than one million dollars when she gives up her career.[5]

Why the huge numbers? After all, women just don't make that much. In 2001, the median annual income for full-time, year-round female workers in the United States was $29,215 ($9,060 less than their male counterparts with similar experience, incidentally).[6] At that rate, even if a woman stayed unemployed for a full seventeen years until her child reached adulthood, she wouldn't get halfway to a million-dollar loss.

To see where all the money's going, one must look beneath the surface and beyond the short term. Many families simply don't consider what they may be losing in insurance, raises, retirement savings, and other benefits when a parent quits or scales back his or her wage-earning work. Retirement income usually takes the biggest hit.

Can I Still Feed Me When I'm Sixty-Four?

How many times have you heard the Paul Tsongas quote *No one on his deathbed ever said, "I wish I had spent more time on my business."*?[7] And everybody reminds you how fast kids grow (as if you hadn't noticed). It's true: Parents who interrupt their earning years to stay home with their children may reap rich emotional rewards even years down the pike. But these parents may also end up in the poorhouse if they don't plan well for retirement.

Social security alone will not provide adequate income for many retirees, especially women. Because today's women retirees have worked fewer years on average than men retirees and earned less when they did work, their social security and private sector retirement savings are also proportionately less. That bad news looks even worse when you realize that women live longer than men and must stretch their meager retirement savings further.

According to the U.S. Social Security Administration (SSA) report "Women and Retirement Security," the median income in 1997 for elderly unmarried women (widowed, divorced, separated, and never married) was $11,161, compared with $14,769 for elderly unmarried men and $29,278 for elderly married couples. The poverty rate among elderly women was 13.1 percent, compared to 7 percent among men. Among unmarried elderly women, the poverty rate was significantly higher: about 19 percent. Elderly unmarried women got 51 percent of their total income from social security. Unmarried elderly men got 39 percent, while elderly married couples got 36 percent. Social security was the only source of income for 25 percent of unmarried women, 20 percent of unmarried men, and 9 percent of married couples.[8]

Private sector retirement plans make up the difference—but when parents have interrupted their working lives and have stopped contributing to employer-sponsored retirement plans during their unemployed years, their retirement savings are smaller. "Among new private sector pension annuity recipients in 1993–94," states the SSA report, "the median annual benefit for women was $4,800," which would cover a year's rent—if rent were four hundred dollars a month. In most parts of the country only subsidized housing is available at that rate. The median benefit received by men during the same time period was $9,600—twice what women got.

Retirement Savings Comparison

	CURRENT AGE	AGES WORKING PART-TIME	AGES WORKING FULL-TIME	RETIRE-MENT AGE	ANNUAL PART-TIME SALARY	ANNUAL FULL-TIME SALARY	ENDING BALANCE
Employed full-time	30		30–59	60		$40,000	$639,800
Employed part-time	30	30–59		60	$20,000		$319,900
Employed full-time with 5-year hiatus	30		35–59	60		$40,000	$464,300
Employed part-time 5 years, then full-time	30	30–34	35	60	$20,000	$40,000	$552,000

Source: Judith Warner, "Why We Work," *Working Mother* (September 2001).

A comparison assembled by *Working Mother* magazine and Ernst & Young shows how today's young woman who does not contribute to a retirement plan while unemployed will reach retirement age with less money to live on. (See the table on the previous page.) This comparison assumes that a woman consistently sets aside 6 percent of her salary in a 401(k) plan and that her employer matches up to 3 percent of her salary. It also assumes a 3.5-percent inflation rate, a 20-percent income tax rate, and investment in stocks earning an average of 8.04 percent.

Ruth Hayden, financial educator and author of *How to Turn Your Money Life Around* and *For Richer, Not Poorer,* is adamant about putting away something for the nonearning spouse's retirement in an account with his or her name on it. She says even twenty-five or fifty dollars a month—or anything up to the limit of three thousand dollars a year—contributed to a retirement account invested in a solid index fund will do. "Budget it right next to your mortgage," Hayden insists. "This is more critical than saving for college. You can borrow for that, but you can't borrow for retirement. Statistics for women in poverty in retirement are horrible."

The statistics and the experts all say the same thing, and they're saying it loudly: If you're paring down expenses to prepare for at-home parenting, *don't skimp on saving for the at-home parent's retirement*—even if it means you must cut some other expense(s) from the balance sheet.

Financial Planning Worksheet

The worksheet on pages 40–42 will help you compare a two-earner household budget with a reduced-income budget.

How to Use the Worksheet

1. Start with the columns labeled "Earner 1," "Earner 2," and "2-Earner Totals" in the income section. Your most recent paycheck stubs should provide the current wage and deduction information you need for each earner. To determine annual wages and deductions, multiply the amount per pay stub in each category by the number of paychecks received each year (twelve if paid once a month, twenty-four if paid twice a month, or twenty-six if paid every two weeks). Now enter any interest, dividends, or capital gains distributions you earn. Finally, enter any other income you receive, such as rent from

rental properties, royalties, or freelance income. To determine your total net income, add your net wages, savings and investment income, and other income.

2. Now fill in the same three columns in the expenses section. Some expenses are work-related while some aren't; some are relatively constant while others may change from month to month. You may have nothing to enter in some categories or may need to add categories that aren't included in the worksheet. Record your current expenses as realistically as possible. This is easy if you've been using a computer program to track expenditures from your checking account. But even if you haven't, you can still gather data about your expenses fairly easily. If you pay for most things by check or debit card, mine your checking account register and/or bank statement for the information you need. For expenses you cover with cash, save receipts for at least a month. Multiply your monthly total or monthly average in each category by twelve to get an annual amount. To determine your total expenses, simply add up all the expenses you've listed.

3. To determine your current cash flow, subtract your total two-earner expenses from your total two-earner net income. If you're following a workable household budget, your current cash flow will be either zero or a positive number.

4. In the column labeled "Changes," enter additions and subtractions to your income and expenses that you expect to make so you can have a parent at home. For example, if you plan to quit your job, enter your net wages as a negative number. This change might put your family in a lower tax bracket. If so, your partner's tax withholding might drop, thereby increasing his or her net wages. Enter that increase as a positive number. If you decide to get rid of your cable TV subscription, enter your annual cable cost as a negative number. If you think your heating bill might go up because you won't turn down your thermostat daily as you do with both parents working outside the home, enter the estimated annual increase as a positive number. If you like, jot an explanatory note beside each change. To compare different scenarios (for example, one full-time and one

part-time earner, two part-time earners, or one full-time earner), photocopy the worksheet and adjust the "Changes" column accordingly for each scenario.

5. Add or subtract the amounts in the "Changes" column from those in the "2-Earner Totals" column to determine your "Revised Totals."

6. To determine your revised cash flow, subtract your revised total expenses from your revised net income. Your goal, of course, is either positive or zero cash flow. You may need to adjust the figures in the "Changes" column to achieve this goal.

Financial Planning Worksheet

	Earner 1	Earner 2	2-Earner Totals	Changes (+ additions -subtractions)	Revised Totals
ANNUAL INCOME					
Wages					
Gross wages					
Deduction: pretax insurance					
Deduction: pretax medical expenses					
Deduction: pretax dependent care					
Deduction: state income tax					
Deduction: federal income tax					
Deduction: other withholdings					
Deduction: pretax retirement plan contributions					
Net wages (gross wages minus deductions)					
Savings and investment income					
Capital gain distributions					
Interest and dividends					
Other income					
Net business income					
Net rental income					
Net miscellaneous income					
Total net income (wages plus other income)					
ANNUAL EXPENSES					
Housing					
Rent					
Mortgage (principal plus interest)					
Homeowner's insurance					
Real estate taxes					
Personal property taxes					

	Earner 1	Earner 2	2-Earner Totals	Changes (+ additions -subtractions)	Revised Totals
Water					
Trash removal					
Natural gas					
Electricity					
Telephone					
Cable					
Internet					
Landscaping and gardening					
Maintenance					
New furniture					
New appliances					
Transportation					
Car payment					
New car fund (savings)					
Fuel					
Maintenance					
Insurance					
Parking					
Bus fare					
Food					
Groceries and liquor					
Family dining out					
Workday lunches, coffee breaks, happy hours					
Medical expenses					
After-tax insurance costs					
After-tax out-of-pocket costs					
Child-related expenses					
After-tax daycare costs					
Tuition					
Diapers and formula					
Uniforms					
Allowance					
Clothing and Personal Care					
Work-related clothing and clothing care					
Hair and skin care					
Other clothing and personal care (all family members)					
Entertainment					
Movies, theater, concerts, CDs					
Date nights					
Baby sitters					

	Earner 1	Earner 2	2-Earner Totals	Changes (+ additions -subtractions)	Revised Totals
Holidays					
Gifts					
Travel					
Entertaining					
Decorating					
Gifts					
Charitable contributions					
Wedding and baby showers					
Birthdays					
Other gifts					
Recreation and hobbies					
Memberships (museum, health club, zoo, and so on)					
Fees for children's lessons, teams, and clubs					
Adult recreation fees					
Supplies and equipment					
Toys and games					
Computers and other electronics					
Vacation					
Transportation					
Lodging					
Entertainment and activities					
Food					
Pet boarding					
Pet care					
Veterinarian					
Food					
Supplies					
Savings and investment expenses					
Emergency savings					
After-tax retirement plan contributions					
College savings					
Stocks					
Other investments					
Miscellaneous expenses					
Household sundries					
Postage					
Office contributions					
Professional associations					
Subscriptions					
Spending money					
Total expenses					
CASH FLOW (+ surplus, - deficit)					

From Two Incomes to One

Planning for Success

Jim Kroening is director of credit counseling services for Family Means, an agency that provides a variety of family social services. Last year Family Means counseled 3,200 families on debt management; 2,400 families are enrolled in a debt repayment program paying back ten million dollars to creditors. Kroening has seen many families with young children end up in debt and desperate because they thought they could shift from two incomes to one without planning for it. He calls this a "head in the sand" problem. "These are folks who have purchased a big, beautiful new home and cars with two incomes. When they have a child and want to stay home, they assume they can make it on one income…. You can't take that chance. You need to get things in order while you're considering staying home."

The biggest trap many of these families fall into, observes Kroening, is using credit cards and home equity loans to make up for a lost salary. "Don't get into the habit of thinking that credit is your income," he warns. "You need to make a serious decision to avoid taking on more debt. I've seen people who have moved from two incomes to one successfully," Kroening says. "But big decisions need to be made."

Here are several suggestions to help you plan a successful one-income lifestyle, compliments of Kroening, other financial counselors, and parents who've been there:

Ten Steps to One Paycheck

1. Start living on just one of your incomes while you're both still employed.

2. Stash the spare income in an emergency savings account for use in case the soon-to-be sole wage earner falls ill or gets laid off.

3. Make sure you have disability insurance and term life insurance for the wage earner in case he or she becomes seriously ill or dies.

4. If necessary, learn how to create and follow a budget with the help of a financial counselor or a budgeting book.

5. Compile an honest list of your current income and expenses. Make your list as complete, accurate, and detailed as possible.

●●●●●●●●●●●●●●●●●●●●

Free Financial Planning Help

The Federal Citizen Information Center (FCIC) is a trusted one-stop source for information on consumer issues and government services. You can view, download, or order dozens of helpful financial publications by visiting the FCIC's web site at http://www.pueblo.gsa.gov and clicking on "Money." If you'd like a free copy of the FCIC's *Consumer Information Catalog*, write to Catalog, Pueblo, CO 81009 or call 888-8PUEBLO (888-878-3256). You can also download or order the catalog on-line at FCIC's web site.

6. Decide which expenses are essential and which are nonessential. Identify nonessential expenses you might trim or eliminate, such as a cell phone, cable or satellite TV, dining out, or expensive hobbies such as golf, antiquing, boating, or wine collecting.

7. Figure out how to pay off or reduce any debt as soon as possible and agree to stop using credit.

8. Compile an honest list of your expected income and expenses with one wage earner and reduced spending and debt.

9. If your projected budget doesn't balance, reexamine your expenses. You may have to make more tough choices, such as whether to downsize your home or own just one vehicle.

10. When you've crafted a livable one-income budget and become comfortable with your new lifestyle, you're ready to cut that second income.

One-Income Living That Works for the Long Haul

Ruth Hayden doesn't mince words: She warns that it isn't easy for a family to live on one income. She speaks from experience; she spent several years at home with her four children before finishing school and starting her successful career in financial consulting, writing, and education.

Hayden has worked with many couples who've wanted to move from two incomes to one in order to have a parent—usually mom, sometimes dad—at home. According to

Hayden, "When women choose to stay home, they do it either for sentimental reasons—because they miss their kids while they're at work—or because they can't afford daycare." They do it "spontaneously and not thoughtfully." She joins the chorus of financial experts who encourage planning ahead for the changes that come with reduced family income. If couples fail to plan, she says, conflict may ensue and result in fighting or even divorce.

According to Hayden, two things are essential to the planning process:

1. Both partners must discuss how their values inform their spending priorities. A family may feel that private school education, organic food, alternative health care, staying in their current house, or tithing to a religious community is very important; any of these values could influence their financial decisions. The couple must then craft a budget that satisfies one or two of their core values. "It has to be one or two, not eight!" Hayden says. "If they pick more than that, it's not going to work." She explains that such priorities must be minimized because everything gets squeezed in a shift to one income. She continues, "They have to agree on this. And they have to be willing to change. They will probably be eating more macaroni and cheese, and their vacation and clothing budget will probably go down." For example, a family's core value might be an annual summer vacation. On one income, they might camp instead of spending a week at a resort.

2. A couple's financial planning must include contributing to an Individual Retirement Account (IRA) for the unemployed partner— still usually a woman. "Something has to be going in a spousal IRA or Roth IRA," Hayden insists, "and that has to be at the top of the budget, or she will get hurt long-term. We've been taught it isn't important [to take care of ourselves financially]. Instead, women tend to spend money to make our homes and ourselves look better, and we spend it on our children. It is our societal training." Hayden notices a sense of empowerment among women who invest in their futures rather than replacing their ratty sofas or buying their kids brand-name clothing. "Something happens to women who take care of themselves," she says. "There is a strength that women have when they know money is accumulating in their own name even while they're taking care of their children."

A No-Fluff Budget

Because Brian, an at-home dad, and his wife, Susie, a software engineer earning about seventy-five thousand dollars a year, have always lived within their means, moving to one income wasn't a huge blow. "We don't have a lot of fluff in our budget," Brian said. They have no cable TV, for example, and live in a modest bungalow in a first-ring suburb of Minneapolis. As a result, they don't miss Brian's forty-thousand-dollar income too much. They have, however, learned to budget more carefully than they used to for big-ticket items. For instance, instead of buying a brand-new minivan, they bought a two-year-old vehicle still in great shape. They also delayed purchasing a new computer for a couple of years while they saved up for it. "With a little patience and planning," Brian says, "we can do the things people do with two incomes."

Trimming Essential Expenses

You've got to have a roof over your head, buy food and clothing, and get away from it all once in a while. Though you really can't eliminate these essentials, you can choose how much you'll spend on them.

Choose Your Housing Carefully

If you're house-hunting, remember that you don't have to take out the biggest mortgage you qualify for. Consider buying a modest house—smaller than you might have imagined, or in a less expensive neighborhood—that you can pay for comfortably. Then get creative and organize your space to make the most of it!

If you already own a home, it may be hard to downsize. But some do: Laurie and Breean of Bellingham, Washington, moved from a renovated farmhouse on a one-acre lot to a house that still has five bedrooms (just smaller) in a city neighborhood a block from their church and their best friends. Breean's law partners may not understand his downward mobility, but he and Laurie see it as a way to shake off the golden handcuffs of his high-salary job. It creates the financial space for him to pursue his career in a way that meshes with his family values. By making this change, Breean can spend less time at work and more time with the couple's three children.

Another money-saving option for homeowners is refinancing. If interest rates are substantially lower now than when you bought your home, and your projected closing costs are lower than your projected savings, you might want to look into this before one of you quits your job. By taking out a new mortgage at a lower rate, you may be able to lower your monthly house payment and/or shorten the term of your loan. Any way you slice it, you could wind up spending a smaller total amount on your house.

A Little Rust Never Hurt Anyone

Though a brand-new car comes with a warranty and an ego boost, it also carries a hefty price tag, and its value quickly depreciates. Consider driving used cars to save on insurance and car payments. If you buy a car that's just one or two years old—perhaps with some warranty remaining—chances are, you'll still get a reliable vehicle at two-thirds to three-quarters of the original cost. You won't have to worry about who's going to inflict that first ding, either!

Even if you must have a second car with a parent at home, you won't be dishing out money for all the costs related to commuting. You may also qualify for a lower insurance rate if you're putting fewer miles on that second car.

Menus and Coupons and Sales, Oh My!

It takes time, but planning your menus and your shopping trips can save big money. Using coupons is a no-brainer. Take it one step further and shop for store specials and economy sizes, then plan your meals accordingly. Many people swear by buying clubs like Costco and Sam's Club, which give you big savings on a variety of items for an annual fee.

The Wheels on the Bus Go All Around

Geri and Bill, a Minneapolis couple with two children ages eight and four, believe that getting by with just one car is feasible in a city with public transportation. Owning one car was part of their decision to live more simply so Geri can be at home with their sons. "Bill buses to work," Geri says, "and he picks his jobs that way."

Maggie and Gerry, a St. Paul couple, also cut back to one car during the years Maggie stayed home with their two small children. In their case, Gerry drove the car to the social service agency where he worked every day, while Maggie bused to the library, the YMCA, and shopping with the children.

My husband used to be paid once a month, and we'd do our grocery shopping for the whole month right after payday—partly to make sure we didn't run out of food money before the next paycheck. We have an extra freezer in our basement, so we'd stock up on sale items and make double batches of soup and spaghetti sauce to freeze. I had to get used to this kind of planning, because left to my own devices, I would've been perfectly content to eat baked potatoes or scrambled eggs for dinner. Now, we plan weekly instead of monthly, and I've come to value the menu posted on the refrigerator, which answers that pesky question *Mom, what's for dinner?*

Many families rely much less on convenience foods like frozen pizza and prepackaged kids' lunches when they make the shift to having a parent at home. Such products may be handy, but they're also expensive. As an at-home parent you might still have days when you're so frazzled, all you can do is dial the phone for takeout. But overall you'll have more time and energy to plan and cook meals. You may even become a master at one-dish Crock-Pot dinners and casseroles, which help you use leftovers and cook in bulk.

Curb Your Appetite for Dining Out

Eating out is often one of the first expenses to get slashed when families tighten their budgets. If you love to dine in restaurants, you don't need to stop entirely, but you'll need to choose when and where more carefully. A couple of "upscale casual" restaurants in my town let kids eat free on certain days. Many Perkins restaurants offer a free child's meal with every adult meal on Tuesday evenings. Maybe go out for pancakes in the morning instead of pasta at night. Instead of a white-tablecloth hot spot, pick a diner with a jukebox; it'll be more kid-friendly anyway. Or pick up some sandwiches at your favorite deli and have a picnic in the park. Perhaps you could make eating out a birthday treat, taking out one child at a time with both parents.

Buy Used

Not only is shopping at garage sales, vintage shops, and thrift stores fun, you can think of it as recycling. If you know where to look in your community, you can find high-quality gently used clothing, furniture, toys, and kid equipment. You'll enjoy bragging about all the bargains you've scored. If you just can't see yourself buying secondhand stuff, you can still take advantage of annual sales at big department stores and outlets.

Revisit Your Vacation Ideas

Hit the Road

Taking a road trip is generally far less costly than flying somewhere and renting a car. To save even more money on a road trip, you can pack a cooler with sandwich fixings, beverages, and a few treats. Then, when you need to stretch your legs and have a meal, you can drive right past the fast-food joints and picnic at a town park or a roadside rest stop.

We also pack Frisbees, baseballs and gloves, and jars of bubbles. Books on tape or music recordings (if you can agree on choices) make the miles go by faster. Once I packed a paper bag for each child with a few small books, toys, and treats I doled out at intervals as incentives for good behavior. It really worked!

Many families with at-home parents say they visit friends and relatives on their vacations instead of going to pricier destinations. One family I know actually took up the offer of everyone who'd ever said casually, "Drop in and see us if you're ever out our way." This family crisscrossed the United States by car one summer, staying with friends and relatives in all corners of the country. The kids met their parents' long-lost friends— and their friends' kids; swam in new rivers, lakes, and oceans; and visited new museums, historic sites, and cities.

Back Yard or Bust

Some families heartily believe that there's no place like home. They spend leisurely vacation time right in their own back yards, doing all the fun things they never have time to do during the daily grind.

Nurture Your Connection with Nature

Other families focus on the outdoors. Camping equipment isn't cheap, but the investment pays off for years and years. And no matter where you're headed, campgrounds are the cheapest lodging you'll find. I'll plug the U.S. National Park Service: Besides clean, well-run campgrounds, they offer incredible vistas and hiking trails, guided walks and talks about historical events, geology, animals, conservation, astronomy...you name it. The United States and Canada are also peppered with some excellent state, provincial, and regional parks.

Cool It on a Weekend Getaway

If camping's not your thing, find a motel with a weekend special and a pool—a sure-fire kid pleaser—and enjoy having someone else make your bed for a weekend.

Low-Cost Everyday Fun

When you take a good look at your budget, you'll probably find that you spend a lot more money than you expected on small day-to-day errands and outings. They don't have the impact of the big purchases—a car, a house, a computer, a major appliance, a family vacation—so they're often underestimated.

What's most fun isn't always what's most costly—just ask any parent who's watched his or her child rip open a gift, then spend hours playing with the box. Nor does making your own fun necessarily mean doing arts and crafts projects that have you awash in glitter and Popsicle sticks, wielding a hot glue gun (unless you live for that kind of challenge).

Making your own fun often means finding it in unexpected places. One friend describes walks around the block that lasted an hour. Each of her boys would lug a plastic pail with him to pick up treasures that he later incorporated into art projects. Other days, they'd draw a line with chalk all the way around the block or stop to watch construction vehicles, her older son's passion during one of his preschool years. Because she had the time—and adjusted her mindset to be patient with her children's agendas—their days together could move at the children's pace.

Here are some more ideas for low-cost everyday fun:

- *Visit a zoo or museum.* With a little up-front investment in an annual membership, you can enjoy endless hours of entertainment at a local children's museum, zoo, art museum, history center, or science museum. Such institutions often offer member discounts on merchandise or classes. If you don't want to pay for a membership, find out if your local zoo or museum has free admission on a certain day.

- *Pack a picnic.* My family has a favorite spot at a park near our home. It's a Japanese garden with a peace bridge, a waterfall, and interesting flowers and trees. From this park we can walk to a lake, a bird sanctuary, and a rose garden. Or we can just toss a ball around or lie on our picnic blanket, staring at clouds.

◉ *Have a family game night.* This works best with older kids, who have longer attention spans (and perhaps, like you, think Candy Land is boring). Uno is one of my family's current favorites. We've also gone through other game phases, including Sorry!, Monopoly, and the card game spoons.

◉ *Party potluck-style.* You know, call up a bunch of people and ask everyone to bring something to share. It's cheap, it's casual, and it can be planned either at the last minute or on a regular basis. My family belongs to a group of friends who meet for a potluck dinner at someone's house on the first Monday of every month.

◉ *Take an Early Childhood Family Education (ECFE) class.* In my state, the school districts sponsor free classes targeted to various groups of parents—for example, those with children of the same age, dads, teen parents, working parents, and so on. Typically, a family attends a two-hour session that includes parent-child interaction time and additional learning opportunities for infants, toddlers, and preschoolers while parents are involved in a discussion group. ECFE classes are great ways to meet other families and learn about your own. They often provide ideas for at-home learning and fun, too.

◉ *Go garage-saling.* When my kids were little, I used to take them to garage sales every Friday. We'd head for neighborhoods where I knew there would be good kids' clothing and equipment to choose from. I'd give each of my children a dollar and let them choose their own "treasures." (Of course, many of these wound up in our own garage sale pile after a while.) As you become an experienced bargain hunter, you'll be able to spot deals on furniture, china, rugs, and other big-ticket items. I recommend shopping kid-free for serious expeditions.

◉ *Treat your sweetie to a cheap date.* You don't have to spend tons of money to have a great time together. Here are several ideas for inexpensive romantic outings:

  ❖ In summer, instead of dining at an expensive restaurant, pack a picnic. Keep it simple: Bring some bread, cheese, fruit, chocolate, and a bottle of wine.

* If the weather's nice, take a bike ride or rent a canoe or in-line skates.

* In winter, go moonlight ice-skating or torchlight cross-country skiing.

* See a matinee movie or find your community's discount theater and take in a second-run or classic film. Stop afterward for ice cream or coffee.

* Put your child to bed a little early and make a nice dinner for just the two of you.

* Plan a breakfast date for a weekend morning. Drop your child off at someone else's house and linger over waffles, lattes, and the newspaper.

* Catch a local act at a coffeehouse. You can enjoy some tasty treats and beverages—as well as some great music in an intimate setting—for less than the cost of one concert ticket or an entrée at a nice restaurant.

* Stimulate your intellects at an author's reading at a local bookstore, university, or writers' center or at a lecture at a local college.

* Save up for a romantic evening by tossing your silver change in a special container every night. When the container is full, go out and have fun spending it on each other. A couple I know collects their change in an old candy tin. When the tin is full, they cash it in at the bank and go on an "hors d'oeuvres crawl." They hop a bus downtown and visit a few places to sample fun drinks and appetizers. They say collecting the money builds anticipation, and that's all part of the fun.

● *Give gifts from the heart.* You may think people equate the cost of your gift with your intention, but this isn't necessarily so. You can give heartfelt, valuable gifts to friends and loved ones without breaking the bank. Here are a few examples—brainstorm some more that fit your particular talents:

* Assemble a coupon book for someone, promising services from the practical (a car wash, baby-sitting, ironing, making a meal,

house cleaning, dog walking, or leaf raking) to the intimate (a back rub, a foot massage…I'll stop there). Kids can do this, too.

❖ Although I enjoy bargain-hunting at secondhand stores, I hesitate to buy secondhand gifts for others because I don't always know if they'll appreciate such finds. But if you know someone who'd treasure a secondhand gift, you'll have no trouble finding unique and inexpensive items, from clothing to jewelry to books to knick-knacks. For example, I once found a gorgeous cashmere sweater in perfect condition for fifteen dollars at a secondhand store.

❖ Do you sew? Make something fun, like a customized apron for someone who likes to cook. Painting smocks and doll clothes make great birthday gifts for kids.

❖ Do you cook? Consider canning or preserving for winter holiday gifts. Who wouldn't like a jar of some lovely salsa, canned garden vegetables, or yummy jam or fruit preserves to bring a taste of summer to the dark days of winter?

❖ Are you handy with tools and wood? If so, you'll probably think of lots of things you can make. For example, how about a custom cribbage board for a friend who likes to play cards? For a child, you could make a set of building blocks or a step stool.

➊ *Plan simple but fun kids' celebrations.* Kids' birthday parties are becoming more extravagant these days. Many parents are willing to shell out big bucks either to do something their child's friends haven't done before or to avoid the hassle of party preparation and cleanup at home. But a kids' party doesn't have to be a big, costly headache. Most kids enjoy low-key get-togethers where they can play games, eat goodies, and go home with little bags of treasures.

➊ *Share magazine or newspaper subscriptions with friends.* And don't forget the public library, where you can borrow CDs and tapes, audio books for long trips, videos, and of course, the latest bestsellers.

A Lean and Meaningful Life
If you decide that your family can make it on one income, bravo! Remember: You're not alone, and it isn't forever. Remember this, too:

Your attitude about your decision can really influence how you cope with your budget-conscious lifestyle.

Sometimes parents who've given up a salary feel deprived and trapped because they've tightened the belt so much, they have to dig for spare change under the car seat to buy a cup of coffee—never mind a new CD or snazzy pair of shoes. In our acquisitive culture, it's hard to resist the idea that having more money means having more freedom.

I encourage you to focus on the aspect of choice instead: Every day, you're choosing to live within your means in order to achieve a goal—being with your kids—that reflects your deepest values. This intentional way of living is hard work, and it doesn't come naturally to most of us; it's a learned behavior and an ongoing process.

The following stories and the resources listed at the end of this book illustrate that there's a whole community of people out there doing the same thing as you—you've just got to seek them out. Living on one income is surely leaner, but it's not necessarily meaner.

One-Income Success Stories

Planning Ahead

Jeanne, an urban planner, and Paul, an environmental engineer, were "more or less equal wage earners," bringing home a hefty combined income before Jeanne quit her job to stay home with their two small children. Losing her paycheck has been "a huge financial loss," Jeanne says. "We can't save at the same rate and we have to be more frugal." They eat out less often and have cut out most clothes shopping—common ways of budget cutting for many one-income families.

More importantly, Jeanne and Paul prepared for their future before they were parents. They made budgeting decisions that in the long run gave them the financial freedom to choose the life they wanted. "We have no outstanding debt other than our house payment. We never did use credit cards," Jeanne explains. "We put money into making extra house payments instead, and now our house is almost paid for."

"We wanted kids earlier," Jeanne says, but she and Paul had struggled with fertility issues. "It's turned out okay because we're in a better position to afford to have an at-home parent now."

One Day at a Time

Martha and Mike also earned equivalent salaries before they had children. Martha worked with adults with developmental disabilities and mental illness. Mike was on the editorial staff of a monthly magazine. Together they brought home about forty thousand dollars a year. Martha continued to work full-time after their first child was born, but when she became pregnant again, she began to consider staying home.

"I think it really scared Mike," says Martha. "He liked the idea, but financially it scared him." Martha credits their success as a stay-at-home family to her courage in keeping the issue on the table, Mike's frugal tendencies, and their shared ability to live within their means.

Because "Mike is so practical," Martha explains, "and I didn't trust myself in managing us on one income, I relinquished all the finances to him and said, 'We'll do it your way.'" Mike's salary has risen over the years, but it's just about the same as their combined income before children.

Like Jeanne and Paul, Martha and Mike have all but eliminated new clothing from their budget—they wear hand-me-downs and shop sales, secondhand shops, and vintage stores. "We drive used cars so we don't have a car payment," says Martha. "These are things that feel smart, but [they're] not the way I was raised."

Their one-day-at-a-time philosophy helps them cope with the difficulties of living within their means and keeps them going

Delayed Childbearing

According to the National Center for Health Statistics, the average age of U.S. women having their first child rose from 21.8 years in 1975 to 24.9 years in 2000. The birth rate (live births per 1,000 women) for women ages 30 to 39 essentially doubled during the same period. For women ages 30 to 34, the birth rate rose from 52.3 in 1975 to 94.1 in 2000. For women ages 35 to 39, the birth rate rose from 19.5 in 1975 to 40.4 in 2000.

In short, women are having children later than they used to. For many, like Jeanne, it's not a choice. But another at-home mom points out, "Having children later in life can be a choice." And she agrees with Jeanne that "that choice can be the means to the end of staying home with children."

Sources: T. J. Mathews and B. E. Hamilton, "Mean Age of Mother, 1970–2000," National Vital Statistics Reports, 51:1 (2002).

J. A. Martin, B. E. Hamilton, S. J. Ventura, F. Menacker, and M. M. Park, "Births: Final Data for 2000," National Vital Statistics Reports, 50:5 (2002).

when times are rough. "On a good day, [my choice to be at home] feels really good. On a hard day, I would really love beautiful new clothes," Martha confides. "But I would much rather be home, so that feeling goes away pretty quickly."

"A lot of people are convinced they can't make it financially," she says. But her family, which now includes three children, is living proof that it's possible to have a stay-at-home parent even on a modest budget.

A Window of Opportunity

Kim and Mark knew they wanted their infant and preschooler to attend private school eventually, and Kim saw a small window of opportunity to be at home with them before she'd *have* to earn money to afford tuition. Kim, an attorney, and Mark, who works in marketing for a major airline, looked at the numbers. They realized that the difference was very small between their two-income budget and a tight but feasible one-income budget that put them in a lower tax bracket and eliminated nanny expenses. By giving up a cell phone, household cleaning help, and vacations and by spending less on hair appointments and clothing for Kim, they made it work.

After two years at home, Kim returned to work at a firm that offered her an 80-percent-time position in education law, a field she enjoys. Her schedule allows her to pick up the kids after school and spend time with them in the evening.

Though Kim sometimes found it difficult financially and emotionally to be at home, she doesn't regret it. She says it relieved both the guilt she'd had while working when her kids were small and the stress of "feeling so rushed all the time."

"I kept telling myself, 'This is a choice I made,'" she reflects. "It was a real adjustment going from one to two kids. I'm so glad I had that time."

One-Plus Income: Working at Home or Part-Time

Being an at-home parent doesn't necessarily mean you don't earn money. If you've tried to craft a one-salary budget and keep coming up short on the income side of the balance sheet, working at home or part-time may be the solution. A growing number of at-home parents are balancing child care and household management with income-producing work by staggering their schedules or freelancing, consulting, or telecommuting. Even the funny pages reflect how traditional at-home parenting is changing: The venerable Blondie is running a catering business from home these days, while Lois of *Hi and Lois* is a real estate agent!

Working at Home

Can It Really Work?

Working at home is the Holy Grail for many parents: It can ease the income crunch, can be sandwiched between family activities and obligations, and is free of work-related evils like commuting and office politics. And yes, many at-home parents really do work successfully at home. (I'm one of them!) But if you're considering working at home, don't be fooled into thinking it'll be easy. As a work-at-home parent, you'll face some of the same balancing issues you may have wanted to avoid by becoming an at-home parent—not to mention some new challenges. See the sidebar at right for a list of questions that can help you determine whether working at home is right for you.

If you can honestly answer "yes" to a majority of these questions—and commit to working toward "yes" on the rest of them—working at home may be right for you.

Are You an Integrator or a Segregator?

Lisa Roberts, an at-home mother of four, is web site director for The Entrepreneurial

Will It Work for You?

1. Are you self-motivated and self-disciplined?
2. Are you enthusiastic and tenacious?
3. Do you have a good attention span and ability to focus?
4. Do you manage your time and space well?
5. Do you know how much time you can realistically commit?
6. Do you know how you'll balance the demands of work and family while you're at home?
7. Can you cope well under stress?
8. Does your family support you?
9. Do you have the equipment and space for a home office?
10. Do you have an aptitude for learning new things?
11. Do you try to improve and educate yourself continually?
12. Can you offer a high-quality product or service at a price people will pay that will make a profit for you?
13. Are you prepared to handle all three main functions of a business (selling, producing, and administrating)?
14. Can you clearly articulate who'll buy from you, how you'll make them aware of you, why they should buy from you and not your competitors, and how you'll deliver your goods or services?

Work-at-Home Essentials

- Designate a room or part of a room in your home as your office. Set up a desk, computer, phone, and so on, and store your supplies and records in this space. Use it as a home base for your work.

- Obtain a cordless phone or a phone headset. Make sure the phone has a "mute" button.

- Consider ordering an extra phone line with a separate number and a custom ring that alerts you to business calls. You can instruct family members not to answer your work phone or custom ring—or at least to greet business callers politely.

- Be prepared to switch gears. You'll either have to ignore the noises outside your office, trusting that your child-care provider or partner is handling things just fine, or you'll have to juggle your professional and parental roles depending on who needs you more at any given moment.

- Set aside a small space in your office where your child can work or play quietly. (Even segregators may need to work with their children nearby sometimes.)

Parent, an organization for parents who want to both raise their children and earn an income at home. She's also the author of *How to Raise a Family and an Income under One Roof* and coauthor of *The Entrepreneurial Parent*, which examines the lives of parents who work at home.

Roberts says there's no typical profession or type of person best suited to work-at-home parenting. She sees all kinds of people in nearly every field of experience making a living freelancing from home. "There aren't a whole lot of boundaries except psychological ones," she says.

She does believe, however, that there are two basic styles of working at home: You're either an integrator or a segregator, and it's important to know which in order to organize your time and space in a way that'll work for you. "An integrator can weave everything together," Roberts explains. An integrator, for example, would allow a child into her office and onto her lap, even while she's on the phone with a client. An integrator is probably good at multitasking. "That's how I operate," Roberts says. "I nursed kids while I was typing. I was pregnant with my fourth one while I wrote my first book. It all was very symbolic." A segregator, on the other hand, separates work time and play time and prefers a more structured schedule and setting. Segregators are either "fully with their kids or fully at work. They secure supplemental child care and have specific [working] hours."

Whether you're an integrator or a segregator, you'll benefit from certain basic tools and ideas. See the sidebar on the previous page for a few tips to get your work-at-home experience off to a smooth start.

What Kinds of Work Do People Do at Home?

Here are some at-home work ideas I've gathered from various web sites, work-at-home parents, and my own experience:

- *Telephone- and computer-based jobs:* These include virtual operators, medical transcribers, customer service representatives, and credit card payment processors. Such jobs generally require that you have a computer and/or telephone system that meets the employer's needs.

- *Direct sales:* It's not just about Avon, Mary Kay, or Tupperware anymore. Direct sales representatives today hawk party supplies, clothing, kids' books and toys, bridal wear, soy candles, bath products, and just about every other product you can imagine. This is an especially good option if you're outgoing and can find a product to sell that you genuinely believe in.

- *Telecommuting:* Some companies that offer telecommuting positions require you to live near their headquarters and apply in person. Telecommuting may also be possible if you're an established, competent, reliable employee and your employer is willing to consider a change in your position. If this sounds like you, be prepared to make a strong case for telecommuting; your boss will probably want assurance about your productivity.

- *Personal services:* Such jobs include tarot readers, psychics, hair stylists, accountants, and tutors.

- *Freelancing:* Market demand can fluctuate and so can your income, but if you're a pro in communications, marketing, or graphic design, chances are you could nab some freelance assignments through word of mouth. Have a great voice? Maybe you could do voiceovers for commercials. Several mothers I know teach music lessons in their homes. Some people get their children into modeling as a way to start a college fund. A growing at-home field is certified personal and professional coaching. This job requires professional training, excellent communication and counseling skills, and a warm telephone manner. Hand modeling? Hmm…maybe not, what with all the diaper changing and dishes.

● *Home child care:* I don't recommend plunging into this unless you're an experienced parent. But if you discover you love the home-based parenting life and love being with children, you might consider getting licensed and soliciting customers. With the right schedule and mix of children, this can be a great way to earn money while spending time with your own kids. Licensing requirements vary from state to state. You may need to take classes in cardiopulmonary resuscitation (CPR) and child development, have your home inspected for safety and make modifications like adding an egress window in a basement or installing child-safety locks on cabinets, or meet other requirements.

● *Piecework:* Sewing, baking, and assembling are some examples of piecework you can do at home. One creative friend of mine hatched the idea of making children's clothes from used adult clothes—a concept she marketed as Recykidables. She eventually sold the brand name when the work volume grew beyond what she wanted to do herself. Another friend bakes a beautiful baguette. When she needs a little extra cash, she puts the word out, takes orders, and— voilà!—homemade bread for her friends' dinner tables, parties, and freezers and money in her pocket.

● *Landlord or caretaker:* My family's duplex experience had its drawbacks—mainly the limited space—but it also had its advantages, most importantly the rental income. Other perks of this lifestyle include being able to pick your neighbors and almost always having an emergency baby sitter on hand. My family of five was finally squeezed out by our need for more space, but for a smaller family, duplex living can be a great way to generate income. Remember: As a landlord, you're responsible for all expenses and maintenance, from a leaky faucet to a new roof. If you're renting, you might find a kid-friendly place needing an on-site caretaker and get a break on your rent in exchange for some upkeep and management work.

Numerous web sites about working at home, including many designed specifically for at-home parents, have surfaced in the past few years. The best of them include reliable and useful information—and even job leads. Some web sites offer member benefits like newsletters, chat rooms, discounts on books or merchandise, and health insurance or other benefits. For a small sample of work-at-home resources available on-line, see the sidebar at right.

Working Part-Time

Another way to ease the income crunch is to work part-time outside the home. An increasing number of families and employers are turning to flexible scheduling as a way to balance work and family.

Jim Kroening is a big fan of tag-team parenting. His wife, a self-employed hairstylist, cares for their three children during the day and works part-time when her husband is home. Kroening admits that this arrangement eats into family time and couple time, but he adds, "That's a choice we've made. And it won't be forever."

Working the night shift may be the answer for parents in round-the-clock careers like manufacturing, nursing, residential social services, and lately, financial services and banking. When Jane, a Denver mom of two and assistant to a bank vice president, wanted to move from full-time to part-time work, she set her sights on the bank's evening and weekend shifts in telephone customer service. She was comfortable taking a job she

Work-at-Home Web Sites

http://www.wahm.com

http://www.work-at-home-index.net

http://www.parentpreneurclub.com

http://www.MomsCareer.com

http://www.moneymakingmommy.com

http://www.hbwm.com

http://www.homeworkingmom.com

http://www.herhomeoffice.com

For hundreds more web sites, just hop on your favorite search engine and type in the words *work at home*.

describes as "quite a few steps below" her previous position because it meant she could put her family first and stay home with her children. "It doesn't bother me," she says. "I can wear jeans and a T-shirt to work and I don't have to pay for parking after hours!" She says working part-time gets her out enough to prevent crabbiness toward her kids—but also enough to remember what a pain working can be.

Working odd jobs is another great way to make some extra cash. My baker friend works occasionally for a caterer. She's on her feet for hours, but helping prepare and serve food at parties puts cash in her pocket and gives her great ideas for her own parties. Another friend of mine served as a contact person for her neighborhood organization. All it required was weekly phone work and delivering lawn signs to neighbors once in a while. Yet another mom I know delivered newspapers on an afternoon route twice a month. And finally, one recent evening I ran into a fellow mom working at a bookstore. Nobody's getting rich doing jobs like these, but they're paying the bills. Furthermore, keeping one foot in the job market can prove valuable when it's time to transition back to full-time employment. (See Chapter 6: Everything Changes for more on this topic.)

Living on Less

Facts about Money

Fact one: Your feelings about money are important.

Did your parents talk about money? Did your family have enough money? Did people in your family argue about money? Your childhood money experiences affect your current financial attitudes—but need not define them. Take some time to sort out your financial feelings; it'll help you gain solid footing on the challenging financial path ahead.

Fact two: "Money is the number-one reason for conflict in a relationship."

Ruth Hayden cites this finding from a 1990s Harris poll in her book *For Richer, Not Poorer*. She became so concerned about it that she began to write and teach about money management for women and couples. If you want to have a parent at home, you have to look at the short-term money issues—how you'll live within your means on a daily, weekly, or monthly basis—as well as at the long-term ones, such as how your decisions will affect your retirement and college savings and your choices about your children's education.

Fact three: No matter how much money you have, you must still decide how to spend it.
It's not a simple equation of more money equals less conflict. No matter how much money a couple has, the partners must agree on how to use it. It's a matter of coming to terms with a budget and coming to agreement on the core values underlying that budget. If your values include having a parent at home with children, you need to make your balance sheet reflect that priority.

The Bottom Line
Living on less than two incomes is difficult. But you can succeed at it if you…

Commit to the value of having a parent at home.
Both parents must believe that the financial sacrifice is worth it. In other words, while you may not be building your bank account in a big way, you're creating emotional capital for your family—and that's a bigger priority.

Communicate about spending priorities.
You can leave the bookkeeping to one parent, but hammering out a budget is a two-parent job. If one of you doesn't buy into the budget, he or she will probably resent the seemingly arbitrary limits. Decide together what you can give up and what you can't afford to leave out of your budget.

Stay open to renegotiating decisions.
Your family's needs and values may change if you have more children, if something unexpected (like illness or job loss) happens, or if your children become passionate about logrolling or accordion playing or some other hobby that requires equipment and travel to competitions. Your budget will work only if it reflects your current needs.

Chapter 3

Caring for Your Child

Learning to Parent

From diapers to driver's licenses, there's a lot to learn about when you're a parent. But no matter how much knowledge or experience you have, you still face this fundamental reality: You cannot control your child. Your child is not an extension of you, so you can't will him or her to do, think, or see one thing or another. What you can control is yourself—how you respond to your child's needs and the kind of home environment you create.

Parenting Immersion

If learning to parent is like learning a new language, at-home parents are enrolled in parenting immersion school. They won't necessarily understand this new language better than or treat their children differently from parents who work outside the home. But at-home parents do spend more time with their children, which gives them more opportunities to observe firsthand what their kids do all day—how they eat, sleep, play, relate to siblings and friends, and express their feelings.

Words of Wisdom

"Your children are not your children. They are the sons and daughters of Life's longing for itself."
—*Kahlil Gibran*, The Prophet

"How difficult it is to be somebody's parent is one of the best-kept secrets around—along with that other one about being somebody's spouse. We all think we're supposed to know."
—*Polly Berrien Berends*, Whole Child/Whole Parent

"[You see] the small ways they develop every day. You know who they are. You don't have to guess," says an at-home mother of two. She goes on to explain that all kids' actions and words must be interpreted within the context of what came before. Being at home gives parents more access to that context and helps them understand and respond to their children accordingly.

For instance, parents of babies must learn to read and respond to nonverbal cues of happiness or distress. It takes practice to figure out that a certain cry means "I'm hungry!" and another means "I need a change of scenery!" Parents of older kids who have lots of contact with peers and other adults must learn how to deal with such outside influences. Again, it takes practice to learn when to listen, when to ask, when to insist, and when to simply hug. The immersion method is an effective way to learn parenting skills, and many find that it paves the way to a lifetime of fluency in the language of family life.

Developing Confidence as a Parent

Standing on Giants' Shoulders

Montessori, Leach, Brazelton, Sears, Dreikurs, Spock…if you don't already recognize the names of these child development experts, you will soon. The roster is long and growing, and every parent has his or her favorite(s). In addition, countless media resources and parent education programs offer child development information and teach strategies for handling issues that tend to arise with children of various ages. And let's not forget the billions of parents who've preceded you. Among them, there are bound to be at least a few who've weathered the same storms as you.

With all these resources available, why reinvent the wheel? It makes sense to choose a few tools from the collective chest of parenting wisdom to help you do your job. Arming yourself with some basic knowledge about child development, discipline techniques, nutrition, and common conflicts between parents and children can help you know what to expect from your child and how to foster his or her growth.

You're the Expert

The sheer volume of parenting information and advice available can be overwhelming. And while there certainly are widely accepted principles that every parent ought to know, there are also plenty of points upon which experts and parents disagree. I think the only absolute truth about parenting is that what works for some families may not work for others. Each family has unique needs, so parents need to weigh their options and then follow their own best instincts.

For me, parenting confidence has come with practice, guided by whatever knowledge and support I've been able to glean from books, experienced parents, and observations of what works and doesn't work with my kids. Over the years, I've become an "expert" on kids…three kids, that is: mine.

A Word on These Words

Like most parents, you want your child to grow up healthy, happy, and successful. And you probably don't need anyone to tell you that striving for these goals through parenting is the most complicated job you'll ever do. You know there's a lot more to it than any book—much less any chapter in a book—could hope to cover. This chapter simply describes some basic child rearing principles and helpful hints that many at-home parents find useful. I hope you'll find that these ideas are handy tools for your own bag of tricks.

Food, Glorious Food

When you're living with kids—especially as an at-home parent—food tends to be the focus of your day…from timing nursing sessions to making sure your older child eats healthy meals and snacks to planning and preparing the family dinner. The amount of time you spend thinking about and dealing with food may amaze you, but look at the bright side: As an at-home parent, you can easily monitor and manage when and what your child eats. The effort you invest will seem worthwhile when you remember that food has a tremendous effect on your child's physical health and even school performance. To put it bluntly, what goes in affects what comes out—in more ways than one.

According to dietitian Bridget Swinney, author of *Healthy Food for Healthy Kids*, many of the major health problems currently plaguing North Americans—obesity, heart disease, high cholesterol, high blood pressure, cancer, diabetes, and osteoporosis, for example—are related to poor eating habits. Swinney explains that these diseases "don't happen overnight, and an occasional splurge is not what causes them. Rather, your frequent or daily habits...over time contribute to or prevent disease. Healthy eating during childhood really can have big payoffs in adulthood"—not only because of the cumulative effects of a prolonged healthy diet, but also because good habits are easier to maintain than to initiate.[1]

Many parents, dietitians, and health care providers believe children's learning ability is closely linked to nutrition. According to the American Dietetic Association (ADA), children who eat breakfast tend to perform better in school,[2] demonstrating "increased problem-solving ability, memory, verbal fluency and creativity."[3] Conversely, children who skip breakfast experience "delayed cognition, particularly regarding the speed of information retrieval in working memory."[4]

The link between behavior and nutrition is more controversial. A 1999 report by the Center for Science in the Public Interest states that seventeen of twenty-three studies show that the behavior of some children with attention deficit/hyperactivity disorder (ADHD) worsens after they eat food with artificial colors or certain commonly allergenic foods such as milk or wheat.[5] But other experts are more cautious about drawing such conclusions. The authors of the American Academy of Pediatrics' (AAP's) *Guide to Your Child's Nutrition* state, "[N]o links have been established between foods and behavior."[6] However, the authors note that if parents observe a connection between their child's diet and unusual behavior, they may choose to eliminate certain foods from their child's diet as long as they offer other choices from the same food group.

Breastfeeding

Breastfeeding is a hot-button issue for many people. The main tension seems to be between "lactivists" (people who actively—sometimes aggressively—promote breastfeeding) and those who feel that such activism causes mothers and babies unnecessary distress. But here's the good news: There's very little debate over the benefits of breastfeeding.

Human breast milk is undeniably the best nutrition for babies—and that's not all. In its policy statement "Breastfeeding and the Use of Human Milk," the AAP explains that breastfeeding provides many health, nutritional, immunologic, developmental, psychological, social, economic, and environmental benefits to infants, mothers, families, and society.[7]

We know breast milk is best for babies. Obstetrician-gynecologist Christiane Northrup explains in her book *Women's Bodies, Women's Wisdom* that breastfeeding is also good for moms. The hormones oxytocin and prolactin produced during breastfeeding help contract the mother's uterus, which encourages the placenta to separate naturally and decreases blood loss,[8] and help a woman return more quickly to her prepregnancy size and weight.[9] Prolactin also induces mothering behavior and milk production, Northrup says.[10] Finally, women who do not breastfeed demonstrate a higher risk for breast and ovarian cancers.[11]

Given the proven benefits of breastfeeding, it makes sense to breastfeed if at all possible. After the often-difficult initial period, breastfeeding is in many ways more convenient than formula feeding because it requires no mixing, heating, or sterilization. Best of all, it's free. And while being at home offers women the distinct advantage of breastfeeding on a natural schedule without the need for pumping, nursing is certainly not limited to at-home mothers. Many a mom who works outside the home is committed to pumping and storing milk so another caregiver can feed her baby breast milk during the workday.

"I can't decide for others," says Geri, who breastfed each of her children well into

Moms Talk about Breastfeeding

For a wide variety of firsthand stories and opinions about breastfeeding, hop on-line and visit http://www.epinions.com/kifm-Health_and_Hygiene_Products-advantages_to_breastfeeding/pp_~1/pa_~1. Epinions.com has retired this discussion, so you won't be able to add your own thoughts to it, but it'll help you look at breastfeeding from many different perspectives.

Breastfeeding Research

Here's a short but powerful excerpt from the AAP's policy statement: "Research...provides strong evidence that human milk feeding decreases the incidence and/or severity of diarrhea, lower respiratory infection, otitis media, bacteremia, bacterial meningitis, botulism, urinary tract infection, and necrotizing enterocolitis. There are a number of studies that show a possible protective effect of human milk feeding against sudden infant death syndrome, insulin-dependent diabetes mellitus, Crohn's disease, ulcerative colitis, lymphoma, allergic diseases, and other chronic digestive diseases. Breastfeeding has also been related to possible enhancement of cognitive development." To read the full document, visit http://www.aap.org/policy/re9729.html.

●●●●●●●●●●●●●●●●●●

Feminism in Its Purest Form

"Thinking that baby formula is as good as breast milk is believing that thirty years of technology is superior to three million years of nature's evolution. Countless women have regained trust in their bodies through nursing their children, even if they weren't sure at first that they could do it. It is an act of female power, and I think of it as feminism in its purest form."

—*Christiane Northrup,*
Women's Bodies,
Women's Wisdom

his second year, "but for me breastfeeding was about more than breast milk being best for the baby." Indeed, breastfeeding enhances attachment between a mother and her baby.[12] In the long run, this connection is likely to create a strong sense of security in the child and satisfaction in the mother, who knows she has given her child the best of herself.

Breastfeeding Letdowns

In general terms, breastfeeding is the ideal infant feeding method. But for some mothers and babies, it may not be the best choice.

Nursing, however natural and beneficial, is often difficult at first. Tender nipples must toughen up to withstand a baby's powerful sucking. Some babies have a hard time latching on and/or sucking properly. Sometimes nursing moms develop mastitis (a breast infection requiring medical attention) or cracked nipples, which can be extremely painful. Developing a feel for when and how long to nurse also takes time. A mother who feels anxious about such obstacles can seek help from a lactation consultant, a pediatrician, an ob-gyn, a nurse-midwife, other nursing moms, or a group like La Leche League (LLL), which promotes breastfeeding and supports breastfeeding mothers.

Breastfeeding can pose psychological as well as physical difficulties. Because newborns feed many times during the day and night, a new nursing mom may feel like a milk machine. The breastfeeding relationship is a pretty exclusive club of two, so she may also feel trapped with or tied down to her baby. As baby develops a predictable routine, mom may be able to plan her days better and perhaps even get some time to herself, but she must still be available at feeding time— or make other arrangements, such as pumping or supplementing with formula. If nursing at bedtime is necessary to help baby sleep, it may be hard for mom to plan an evening out with her partner or friends. For problems like these, mom may find that other nursing mothers provide the best ideas and support.

Perhaps the biggest drawback of breast-feeding is that only one parent—mom—can do it. Dads of breastfed babies (especially stay-at-home dads flying solo) may experience keen frustration when they can't satisfy their children's hunger quickly and easily. Using a high-quality breast pump is a workable solution for many families. Mom pumps milk from her breasts directly into bottles, then stores it in the refrigerator or freezer to be warmed and used when necessary.

Some parents find that introducing a bottle early (around four weeks) gets babies to realize that food may come from other sources than breasts. Some infants stubbornly refuse bottles; others take them with little difficulty. Milk flows faster from a bottle, which can be a blessing or a curse. The faster flow may help make up for the absence of mom's warm, soft breasts and her unique voice, smell, and touch—but on the flip side, some babies boycott the breast after discovering that bottle feeding is easier.

Your Local La Leche League

- Visit http://www.lalecheleague.org/WebIndex.html to find a group near you that has a web site.
- Check the white, yellow, and blue pages of your local telephone directory. If there's no listing under *La Leche League,* look under *breastfeeding, lactation, community resources,* or *women's health.*
- Call your health care provider. Many keep a file of LLL leader names. Your local library may also have a list.
- In the United States, call 800-LALECHE or 847-519-7730. In Canada, call 800-665-4324 (or 514-LALECHE for French speakers).

••••••••••••••••••••

The View from a "Breastfeeding" Dad

Paul occasionally cared for his newborn daughter, Meg, while his wife, Kelly, got out for an hour or two during her twelve-week parental leave. Meg refused to take a bottle from him. "It was very stressful," says Paul. "You understand how people cross the line. I consider myself a reasonably calm individual, and I ended up *yelling* at Meg. Kelly would come home, and Meg would nurse and be fine, and she'd be like, 'What's the big deal?'"

"I didn't expect [being home with Meg] to be hard for me," said Paul, who believed what he'd read in LLL materials about the advantages of breastfeeding. But after experiencing the difficulties described above, he says, "I thought it was disappointing and insulting that they didn't talk about the partner." He thinks it's important for both nursing moms and their partners to be aware of problems and frustrations the partner may encounter.

The beginning of Paul's parental leave with Meg, then three months old, was rough because Meg had previously rejected the bottle. "There was a lot of stress and tension on my part," Paul says. But by "noon or one o'clock" on the first day of Paul's leave, Meg finally took a bottle of breast milk. "The first week was a big deal about feeding. But it began to mellow out after a couple of weeks, and that's when it started getting fun."

Beyond Breastfeeding

Nutrition Nuggets

I certainly can't tell you everything you need to know about children's nutrition in these few pages, but I can point you in the right direction with some basic guidelines[13] and a few tips from my own experience.

Following the daily serving guidelines shown in the U.S. Department of Agriculture's (USDA's) Food Guide Pyramid for Young Children will help you plan your preschooler's meals and snacks and ensure that your child gets the nutrients and energy needed for proper growth and development. Serving sizes depend on the food and the child's age. The sample servings listed below are appropriate for children ages four to six.

- The *grain* group provides vitamins, minerals, complex carbohydrates, and dietary fiber. Some healthy examples are rice, whole-grain bread and crackers, bulgur wheat, oatmeal, cold unsweetened cereal, pasta, pancakes, tortillas, taco shells, bagels, and pretzels. Young children should have six servings per day. A serving might be one-half slice of bread, one-half cup cold cereal, three to four crackers, or one-third cup rice.

- The *vegetable* group provides vitamins, minerals, and dietary fiber. Some examples are carrots, celery, broccoli, spinach, cucumbers, tomatoes, mustard, collard and turnip greens, green beans; and starchy vegetables like corn, plantains, sweet potatoes, potatoes, and green peas. Young children should

have three servings per day. A serving might be one-half cup
chopped raw or cooked vegetables or one cup leafy greens.

- The *fruit* group also provides vitamins, minerals, and dietary fiber. It
includes fresh fruits like bananas, apples, oranges, mangoes, papayas,
berries, kiwi fruits, grapes, and watermelon; dried fruits like raisins;
canned fruits like chopped pineapple; cooked fruits like applesauce;
and fruit juice. Young children should have two servings per day.
A serving might be one-half piece of fresh fruit, one-third cup
juice, or one-fourth cup canned fruit.

- The *milk* group provides calcium. Some examples are cheese, yogurt,
ice cream, milk, soy milk, cottage cheese, and pudding. Young children should have two servings per day. A serving might be one-half
cup milk, one ounce cheese, or one-half cup yogurt.

- The *meat* group provides protein, iron, and zinc. Some examples are
eggs, dry beans and peas, peanut butter, tofu, soy meat, beef, pork,
sliced lunch meat, poultry, and fish. Young children should have two
servings per day. A serving might be one egg, one-third cup cooked
dried beans, or two one-inch cubes of meat.

- *Fats and sweets* should be limited, though children do need some fat for
early growth and development. By age five they should be getting just
30 percent of their total daily calories from fats—the same as adults.

Children ages two to three need the same number of servings as four-to-
six-year-olds, but the servings may need to be smaller—about two-thirds
as big. The milk group is an exception; two-to-three-year-olds need a full
two servings per day from this group.

Children older than age six need more servings from all the food
groups. They need six to eleven servings from the grain group, three to
five servings from the vegetable group, two to four servings from the fruit
group, two to three servings from the milk group, and two to three servings from the meat group. Fats and sweets should be limited. The size of
servings can be the same as the size of servings for four-to-six-year-olds.

Remember that variety is key and that all five major food groups
(not including fats and sweets) are equally important. The following strategy will help you reach your child's nutrition target each day: For breakfast and lunch, offer foods from three of the major groups. For dinner,

Food Tips for Tots

- Some foods are choking hazards for children ages two to three. If you have a child this age, watch your child eat and avoid serving hot dogs, popcorn, peanut butter, whole grapes, nuts and seeds, chips, pretzels, marshmallows, raisins, raw carrots or celery, and round hard candies—or cut these foods into manageable pieces. By age four most children can chew and swallow well.

- When you introduce new foods, offer one to two tablespoons at first to avoid waste. If your child wants more, he or she will ask.

- When you buy juice, read the label to make sure you're getting 100 percent fruit juice without added sweeteners.

- Let your child help choose and prepare foods to engage his or her interest in eating them.

- If your child is one to two years old and drinking cow's milk, make it whole milk. Switch to low-fat or skim milk when your child turns two.

offer foods from four groups. For each snack, offer foods from two groups.

Eating well is vital to a child's physical development and overall health. One reason to be especially conscious of nutrition: American children today are notoriously overweight. According to the ADA, during the 1990s the number of children who were overweight more than doubled. Approximately 11 percent of American children were overweight, and an additional 14 percent had a body mass index between the eighty-fifth and ninety-fifth percentiles, which put them at increased risk for becoming overweight.[14] During the same period a study of children with diabetes indicated that the number of kids with type 2 diabetes (the kind usually associated with obesity) rose from 4 percent to approximately 20 percent.[15] This is arguably the result of too little robust physical activity and too much junk food.

As an at-home parent, you're in a great position to keep fast food and junk food out of your family's life and put real food in! You can also rely less on processed convenience foods and do more of your cooking from scratch. I used to be happy to stir a can of cream of mushroom soup into a casserole until my husband taught me how to make white sauce from flour, butter, and broth. It's not much harder than opening a can. You can use low-sodium canned broth or make your own, which is really quite simple and reduces salt and preservatives. (See the recipe on the following page.)

Though managing your child's diet may be easier for you than for a parent who works outside the home, you'll probably still battle over food sometimes. You may find yourself insisting (perhaps just like your own mom or dad), "Clean your plate!" or, "Eat your broccoli!" I recommend avoiding power struggles over food if you can. Experts say that kids will eat what they need when offered a balanced diet, and that power struggles over food can lead to eating disorders. Besides, kids' tastes tend to vary widely from day to day. It's normal for a child to develop a sudden distaste for something he or she loved last week (or vice versa).[16] [17]

Patient parents can promote healthy eating by setting a good example for their kids and persistently offering new foods. "With a minimum of eight to ten exposures to a food, children will develop a clear increase in preference for that food," says the ADA. "Thus, parents and other child caregivers can provide opportunities for children to learn to like a variety of nutritious foods by exposing them to these foods."[18]

Produce Pointers

We're all supposed to eat at least five servings of fruits and vegetables every day. They're packed with the vitamins, minerals, and fiber we need for daily functioning.[19] Many are also rich in antioxidants, which combat cancer, heart disease, diabetes, and dementia, among other illnesses.[20] Encourage your child to pick out a new fruit or veggie each week at the grocery store, then try it together! My local food co-op's newsletter recently highlighted a few star performers:[21]

Simple Homemade Chicken Broth

Whenever you cook a chicken, throw an extra pan on the stove and make this broth to use for another meal. I learned this trick by watching my father-in-law make turkey soup with the leftover carcass every Thanksgiving.

Miscellaneous chicken parts (wingtips, tail, backbone, gizzard, liver, and so on)
onion, quartered
carrot, cut in big chunks
celery rib, cut in big chunks
Coarsely chopped celery leaves (optional)
Peppercorns and salt to taste

1. Put the chicken parts in a saucepan. Add onion, carrot, and celery. Add a few peppercorns and salt to taste. (I use about 1 teaspoon salt and 4 peppercorns.)
2. Cover the chicken and veggies with water. Heat the mixture to a rolling boil, then simmer it on low heat for 30 to 45 minutes.
3. Strain the broth into jars and store it in your refrigerator (if you'll be using it within a few days) or freezer.

The Parents' Ten Commandments of Healthy Eating

1. Thou shalt not force or bribe thy child to eat.
2. Thou shalt set a good example by eating at least five fruits and vegetables and drinking three glasses of milk per day thyself.
3. Thou shalt make mealtimes pleasant.
4. Thou shalt encourage thy child to help in meal planning, preparation, and cleanup.
5. Thou shalt back off when mealtime becomes a power struggle.
6. Thou shalt accept food jags as phases that will eventually pass.
7. Thou shalt accept the fact that thy child is an individual and thus will dislike certain foods. (And there may be many!)
8. Thou shalt not give up on introducing thy child to new foods. Thou shalt realize it sometimes takes ten tries to get a child to accept a food.
9. Thou shalt use this division of responsibility for eating: As the parent, thou art responsible for deciding when to eat and what to serve. Thy child is responsible for deciding how much (if any) he will eat.
10. Thou shalt give thy child a multi-vitamin-mineral supplement if he is a picky eater.

Source: Bridget Swinney, *Healthy Food for Healthy Kids*, Meadowbrook Press (1999): pp. 5–6.

Cruciferous vegetables: Broccoli, cabbage, Brussels sprouts, cauliflower, and kale, for example, cut the risk of some cancers.

Apples and apple juice: These kid favorites help prevent clogged arteries.

Prunes: Okay, here's a true confession…. One of my earliest memories is of my mother passing me a glass of prune juice around the bathroom door when I was constipated! Let's rescue prunes from their reputation as bowel cleansers—there's so much more to them! They're sweet and chewy. And they're highest in antioxidants of fifty fruits and vegetables measured in a Tufts University study.[22] (Others that are high in antioxidants are raisins, blueberries, kale, and spinach.)

Greens: These leafy delights are rich in bone-strengthening vitamin K. Salad may be an acquired taste; not many kids are salad lovers. But try creamy buttermilk or tahini dressings and see if your child bites.

Carrots: Here's another kid pleaser with tons of beta-carotene, which keeps colds at bay and may cut the risk of heart disease and breast cancer. Try sautéing carrots for five to seven minutes with a little butter, then sprinkle them with cinnamon and ground ginger. Yummy!

Organic Produce

There's no denying organic produce costs more than conventionally grown produce. But is it worth the expense?

Eating any fruits and vegetables is better than eating none, but organic produce may indeed be better for both you and your child. According to a report published by the National Academy of Sciences, "pesticides can cause a range of adverse effects on human health, including cancer, acute and chronic injury to the nervous system, lung damage, reproductive dysfunction, and possibly dysfunction of the endocrine and immune systems."[23] Pesticides are particularly risky for children because their organs and systems are still developing.[24]

We've known about the risks of pesticides for decades; hasn't this problem been addressed already? Well, yes and no. Food safety research and regulations are indeed improving in the United States—but pesticides are still out there. Studies conducted independently by Consumers Union, the USDA, and the California Department of Pesticide Regulation all show that conventionally grown produce is three times as likely to contain pesticide residues as organic produce.[25]

Washing produce gets rid of only about one-third of pesticides on the surface. Peeling may further reduce the amount of pesticide in a piece of produce, but also robs it of the most concentrated source of nutrients. According to the Environmental Working Group (EWG), a nonprofit research organization that analyzes databases from state and federal government agencies like the Food and Drug Administration, produce containing the most pesticides—and the most toxic ones—are bell peppers, spinach, cherries, cantaloupe, apples, apricots, green beans, grapes, cucumbers, U.S.-grown strawberries, peaches grown in Mexico, and celery from Chile. There are several kid favorites on this list! If you can only afford a few organic items, maybe these should be the ones.

EWG also notes that some conventionally grown fruits and vegetables, such as bananas, pineapple, watermelon, plums, blueberries, grapefruit, avocados, cauliflower, radishes, broccoli, onions, okra, and cabbage are consistently low in pesticides.

Smart Snacks

For Toddlers

- Cheerios or any breakfast cereal that's not too sugary
- Graham crackers: plain or dipped in vanilla yogurt
- Crackers or apple slices with peanut butter
- Pretzels
- Fruit
- Yogurt

For Older Kids

- Ants on a log: celery sticks filled with peanut butter or cream cheese and topped with raisins
- Tortilla chips and salsa
- Carrot sticks, celery sticks, and/or cucumbers with veggie dip
- Corn bread: yummy heated up with a bit of butter and honey
- Cheese pizza: Cooking tomatoes (as in pizza sauce) with fat (such as oil or cheese) unleashes large amounts of the cancer-fighting antioxidant lycopene.[26] It doesn't take a lot of fat to deliver the goods, so there's no need to pile on the cheese, sausage, and pepperoni—a low-fat veggie pizza will do the trick, too!
- Fruit
- Whole-wheat crackers with goat cheese: Use herbed spread for a savory flavor or plain spread with a dash of fruit preserves for a sweet flavor.
- Yogurt
- Popcorn: Bypass the microwave and pop it yourself on the stovetop or in an air popper—it's tastier, more fun, and less processed.
- Toast with peanut butter and raisins

Kids in the Kitchen

Parents often have more time to cook when they move to the home front, and it can be fun to let the kids help. Most kids enjoy measuring, pouring, and stirring with help from mom or dad. Simple baked goods like corn bread, banana bread, and drop cookies are great to make with kids. Kids can also help sprinkle cheese on casseroles, snap green beans, husk corn...there are lots of suitable jobs, even for small children.

Pizza Dough

Asked to rate frozen, takeout, and homemade pizza, my kids rank homemade first. Our favorite pizza dough recipe, which makes two twelve-inch or four eight-inch crusts, is below. Making pizza dough is both fun and educational for kids. You can explain that the yeast is a living creature that eats sugar and makes carbon dioxide (the same gas people exhale), which creates bubbles in the dough that make it rise.

- 3½ cups unbleached all-purpose flour
- 1 teaspoon salt
- 1 package (2½ teaspoons) active dry yeast
- ½ teaspoon sugar
- 1¼ cups warm water (If it feels pleasantly warm but not hot on the inside of your wrist, it'll work.)
- 2 tablespoons olive oil

1. In a food processor fitted with a chopping blade, pulse the flour and salt briefly to combine them.
2. Dissolve the yeast and sugar in the water. Let the mixture stand 5 minutes or until it's foamy. Add the olive oil.
3. Switch on the food processor and pour in the yeast mixture in a steady stream. Keep processing until the dough forms a ball on top of the blade. (If the dough doesn't form a ball, it's too dry. Add cold water 1 tablespoon at a time until a ball forms. If the dough seems sticky, it's too wet. Add flour 1 tablespoon at a time until the dough is moist but not sticky.)
4. Process the dough for 45 more seconds to knead it. Put it in a lightly oiled bowl and cover it tightly with plastic wrap. Let the dough rise in a warm, draft-free place for about 20 minutes or until it doubles in volume. It's ready when you can poke a finger in it and leave an imprint.
5. Punch the dough down, roll it out, add your favorite toppings, and pop your pizza in the oven.

Source: Irena Chalmers, *The Working Family's Cookbook.*

If you just can't stand to relinquish control of your cooking, provide kid-size utensils and bowls and let your child mix up his or her own concoctions as you work. And remember how much kids like bubbles—let them help you do the dishes!

My three kids need packed lunches five days a week, so they make their own as often as possible. This not only gives them the power to decide what they'll eat (within parental guidelines, of course), it also helps them realize that meals don't appear magically—someone has to plan and make them every day. If your child eats a packed lunch, suggest these easy, tasty ideas:

- Peanut butter is a staple in my house. It's quite nutritious—especially the natural kind with no added sugar. Natural peanut butter costs more and isn't widely available in big tubs, but you can buy it in bulk at many food co-ops. My children probably make peanut butter and jelly or peanut butter and honey sandwiches for lunch about half the time. For variety, try apple slices (sprinkled with lemon juice to prevent browning) with a small container of peanut butter and a plastic knife.

- Here's a homemade version of the prepackaged lunch: In separate containers and/or Ziploc bags, pack a few crackers, quartered cheese slices, quartered pieces of lunch meat, and applesauce or chopped pineapple. Add a juice box or skim chocolate milk.

- Make a hearty soup for dinner and double the recipe so you have leftovers. Heat it up in the morning and pour it in a small Thermos. Many kids like vegetable soup, minestrone, chili, and creamy chowders and puréed soups.

- A bagel with cream cheese is nutritious, filling, and can be prepared in less than two minutes.

- For a fast dose of veggies, keep a bag of peeled, washed baby carrots on hand.

- Many single-serving foods are available in stores, but you can reduce waste—not to mention save money—by buying economy sizes and filling small reusable containers instead. My kids do this a lot with pineapple canned in its own juice and applesauce topped with cinnamon. Canned peaches and pears and fresh cantaloupe and grapes are other kid favorites. Kids can also pack cereal in a bowl-size plastic container and add milk at school. (Don't forget a spoon!) Containers come in an infinite variety of shapes and sizes; you can even buy a lunch box with custom-fit containers and a Thermos.

As an at-home parent you might also have time to tend a vegetable/herb garden with your child. Kids love chives, tomatoes, pumpkins, green beans, and radishes—things that grow quickly and/or can be tasted fresh-picked. You could give your child a small plot in which to plant whatever he or she wants.

Learning and Playing

The most important way children develop their physical, cognitive, and psychological skills is by doing what they love to do most: play! For years my son loved building with Legos and acting out scenes with Star Wars figures. My younger daughter loves her baby doll. Her sister plays school or dress-up games in which she and her friends imagine themselves as other characters.

Over the years I've come to believe that kids probably need fewer toys than we think they need. For babies, parents are the best toys of all. Your baby loves to be near you, see your face, and watch you work. Children naturally add toys to their repertoires as they grow, but the toys needn't be complex or expensive. The book *Whole Child/Whole*

Share Your Passions

Whether your passion is play dough or Pavarotti, being at home gives you more time and energy to share it with your child. Mark, who loves fly-fishing, takes his kids angling in a canoe on summer days at a city lake just five minutes from home. Geri, an artist, makes sculptures with the treasures her kids bring home from walks and helps them transform appliance boxes into castles, houses, and other buildings with paint. Chris, a competitive swimmer and triathlete, swims with his four-year-old son almost daily. Martha, an actor, says, "One thing that really grounds me with my kids is reading. It reminds me of when my mom read to me, and I'm a good reader! They just love it."

Parent by Polly Berrien Berends describes many simple toys you can buy or make that help kids develop a foundation for future abstract thinking, such as geometric concepts like parts and wholes and the elementary physics involved in construction. Of course to a child, these toys are just toys—building blocks; puzzles; simple manipulatives that nest, stack, or link together; and natural materials like water, sand, and dirt.[27]

Tried and True Toys, Games, and Activities

- *Nesting cups:* These are great for the sandbox and bathtub, and somehow they hold kids' interest for years.
- *Sandbox and assorted containers and utensils:* There's no need to buy special sand toys; just use old kitchen things.
- *Bubbles*
- *Sidewalk chalk*
- *Jump rope*
- *Kite*
- *Lemonade stand:* Let kids mix lemonade from concentrate and hawk it from a little table in front of your home. Keep a close eye on the customers who stop by.
- *Playing cards:* Use them to play go fish, concentration, spoons, war, or whatever games your family loves.
- *Back yard volcano:* Make a play dough mountain with a hole in the middle. Put some baking soda in the bottom of the hole, fill it with vinegar, and stand back. *Whoosh!*
- *Dress-up wardrobe:* Hit garage sales and buy a variety of hats, dresses, pants, shirts, scarves, ties, and jewelry. Stash it all in a clear plastic storage tub with a lid. (This makes an excellent gift for a child, too!)
- *Play dough:* If you've got a few spare minutes, you can skip the store-bought stuff; this is easy to make! (See the recipe on the next page.)

Children's Work

The flip side of playing is what Montessori educators call children's work—the repetition of practical life tasks. Children allowed to practice such tasks with appropriate-size materials develop self-esteem, independence, and a sense of purpose while learning that they can contribute to the household.

Play Dough

"Think about play dough and its calming properties. You know how we're all looking for quality time with our kids? Well, how about this very old idea? Mix up some play dough. Play with it at the kitchen table. Maybe play some music in the background. Take the time that is needed for this project. Don't have [your kids] play...while you get your three thousand tasks done. There's plenty of time to do that kind of thing.... Here's the recipe:

2   cups flour
1   cup salt
4   tablespoons alum
2   teaspoons vegetable oil
2   cups water
2   drops food coloring

Mix all ingredients together.... Stir over medium heat until a ball forms."

Source: "The MOMbo Moment," *MOMbo* radio program, (aired November 14, 2001).

Do it myself! is often a child's mantra by age two or three. In the early 1900s, Italian physician Maria Montessori developed an educational method based partly on the premise that children *should* do as much as possible for themselves—as early as possible—and that adults should create environments that nurture this impulse.

Current research on brain development validates many of Montessori's ideas. A *Time* magazine article on early childhood brain development says that "[p]sychiatrists and educators have long recognized the value of early experience," but their claims have been backed largely by anecdotal evidence. Now, however, "modern neuroscience is providing the hard, quantifiable evidence that was missing earlier."[28] In a nutshell, both the soft and hard evidence indicate that the minds of children from birth through age six are, as Montessori described, incredibly "absorbent." Children of this age are not only at the peak of their natural ability to acquire language, they are also developing brain activity patterns for hand-eye coordination, visual acuity, and emotional health.[29]

Fostering Independence

Small Kid + Small Job = Big Deal

It takes extra time, planning, and patience to let children—especially very young ones—groom themselves and do household chores, but it's important to encourage them to master such tasks. For example, you can't make a

Age-Appropriate Chores

2 to 3 Years

- Throw things in trash
- Get things when asked
- Pick up and put away toys with help
- Wipe up spills
- Put dirty clothes in hamper
- Hang clothes on hooks
- Mop small area with child-size mop
- Pour from small pitcher kept on low shelf in refrigerator
- Hand dishes from dishwasher to parent

3 to 4 Years

- Do above tasks
- Help set table by handing silverware to adult
- Clear dirty dishes
- Hold dustpan
- Empty small wastebaskets
- Close drawers in bedroom
- Put away clean clothes without help

4 to 5 Years

- Do above tasks
- Help fold clean clothes
- Set out clothes, backpack, and so on for next day
- Use hand-held vacuum
- Water houseplants
- Unload utensils from dishwasher
- Help wash dishes
- Fix bowl of cereal
- Make bed without help
- Help put away groceries

peanut butter and jelly sandwich quickly if you let your three-year-old help, but your child will be very proud of contributing to the meal and will exercise fine motor control and hand-eye coordination.

To create an environment that fosters a preschooler's independence, your home could reflect certain aspects of a Montessori classroom. You might install hooks for outerwear, storage cubbies, and mirrors at your child's level (or at least accessible with an easily movable stool). You could also buy pint-size but functional tools like mops, brooms, and gardening equipment.

After you've taught your preschooler how to do various self-care and household tasks, let him or her do as much as possible independently. Encourage your child to ask for help from a parent or older sibling if necessary. But if your child misses a blob of jelly on the table or buttons a shirt lopsided, so what? He or she is probably very proud of the accomplishment, and hasty criticism from beloved mom or dad might cause shame or even anger. Small successes—however imperfect—breed confidence. (And hey, adults make mistakes in this area, too: I've been known to appear in public with mismatched socks or my sweatshirt on backward!)

The sidebars on pages 84–86 will give you an idea of what your child may be able to do at various ages.

Taking Wing

Toddlers and preschoolers encouraged to develop independence through self-care and household tasks usually continue to self-direct in these areas as they grow older. These kids feel good about contributing to the household and family, and they look forward to the privileges that accompany growing independence. Elementary-age children may push for greater freedoms like permission to ride a bike alone in the neighborhood or to go to the library, a movie, or the playground with a friend. Preteens and young teens may want to hang out at the mall unsupervised, try trendy clothing and hairstyles, or watch movies rated PG-13 or even R. Many children understand that they can earn parental trust—and a shot at the freedoms they desire—by showing a good track record of doing their homework, completing assigned chores, cleaning their bedrooms, managing their personal belongings, and so on.

Balancing privilege with responsibility is an important parental task, and decisions on such matters can vary widely depending on parents' values and comfort with their children's growing independence. For example, a couple of years ago one of my daughter's friends came over to play. I let the girls bike around our block together. The next time this friend visited, her mother asked me not to let them go around the block alone, as her husband had been quite uncomfortable thinking of his eight-year-old unaccompanied in an unfamiliar neighborhood. I appreciated her honesty and respected her wishes, and the girls and I took our dog for a walk together instead.

5 to 6 Years
- Do above tasks
- Help change bed linens
- Help sort laundry
- Sort recycling
- Help prepare meals, peel vegetables
- Feed pet
- Help clean pet's litter box or cage

6 to 7 Years
- Do above tasks
- Sweep floors
- Help make and pack lunch
- Help with yard work
- Pour own drinks
- Answer phone
- Bathe in tub filled by parent

7 to 8 Years
- Do above tasks
- Help with grocery shopping
- Wash, dry, and put away dishes without help
- Wash table after meals
- Fill and empty dishwasher
- Make own snacks

8 to 9 Years
- Do above tasks
- Sew buttons
- Run bath
- Cook simple food (such as toast)
- Mop floors
- Pack suitcase

10 to 12 Years

- Do above tasks
- Prepare simple meals or box mixes
- Use washer and dryer with help
- Straighten rooms
- Clean bathroom
- Wash windows
- Wash car
- Iron clothes
- Baby-sit younger siblings (with adult present)
- Mow lawn
- Clean kitchen
- Plan birthday party
- Have neighborhood job (such as pet care, yard work, or paper route)
- Shovel snow

13 Years and Older

- Do above tasks
- Clean garage and basement
- Plan menus, prepare and serve meals
- Baby-sit younger siblings without adult present
- Change light bulbs
- Replace vacuum bag
- Clean refrigerator
- Make grocery list

Older and Wiser

Discussions about independence between older teenagers and their parents may include more complex topics like dating, driving, curfews, or college visits. Many parents continue to link privilege with responsibility. For instance, using the family car might depend on getting good grades or chipping in for car insurance. One mother said that her high school–age son's privilege and responsibility were one and the same: She decided to let him handle his own schedule. He could choose and plan all his own extracurricular activities as long as he wrote them on the family calendar and arranged for a ride if needed. After missing a few sports practices, he realized that he really was in charge—which increased his sense of control over his life and decreased his mom's stress level.

An older teen may seek an after-school, weekend, or summer job, which is another step toward greater responsibility and freedom. Some appropriate jobs for teenagers are baby-sitting, pet-sitting or pet care, refereeing or coaching for a children's sports league, lifeguarding, and counseling at a summer camp. Retail and fast-food jobs may be right for some teens, but families should make sure that the working hours don't interfere with homework, family life, and adequate sleep.

An Allowance Allows Growth

Having a part-time job and a paycheck is a great way for a teen to develop self-confidence, responsibility, and independence. But a kid can gain experience handling money and making spending choices even earlier if his or her parents offer an allowance.

There seem to be two schools of thought on allowances: An allowance is either a payment for performing household chores or an unearned right. Both approaches have merit. If you want to investigate them more closely, there are many books, web sites, and magazine articles that treat the subject thoroughly.

No matter how you look at it, an allowance can be a great tool for teaching money values. A pocketful of jingling coins or crisp bills can do wonders to help a kid feel grown-up. And being responsible for saving and spending money is a good introduction to the world of "taxes and insurance" (my kids' shorthand for the boring but necessary details of personal finance that seem to monopolize adult conversation).

Many families I know require their children to designate some of their allowance for savings, some for charitable contributions, and the rest for discretionary spending. If your child has a weekly or monthly allowance (or earnings from a job), he or she should have a say in how it is spent. Managing a small amount of money now is a great way to learn how to make wise financial decisions: "Do I buy the double-scoop ice cream cone now or save up and buy the newest book in the Magic Tree House series next week?" "Do I spend my baby-sitting cash on that Dixie Chicks CD today or amass big bucks for buying souvenirs on our family vacation?" "Do I stop by Starbucks every day or stash the cash in my college fund?" You get the idea!

Screen Time versus Story Time

Screen Time: The Problem with TV

It's easy to rant about TV, especially after reading all the research on TV and children's behavior and health. One report shows a direct link between TV viewing and violent or aggressive behavior in children.[30] Excessive TV viewing is not only linked to increased violence, it's inversely related to good reading scores, has a negative effect on cognitive brain development,[31] and promotes obesity,[32] which is the number two cause of preventable death in the United States.[33] The more TV children watch, the more likely they are to snack between meals, eat foods advertised on TV, and try to influence their parents' food purchases. Well over half the ads

TV Rx

The American Academy of Pediatrics (AAP) recommends no more than one to two hours of quality TV and videos a day for children older than two years and no screen time at all for children under the age of two.

Source: "Children, Adolescents, and Television," policy statement reported in *Pediatrics*, 107:2 (Feb. 2001): pp. 423–26.

shown on Saturday mornings are for high-sugar, high-fat foods like breakfast cereals, cookies, candy, and fast food. (One study documented 202 ads for junk food during four hours of Saturday morning cartoons.)[34][35] Children in food commercials are almost always shown eating with other children or alone—rarely with their parents. "The diet depicted in Saturday morning television programming is the antithesis of what is recommended for healthful eating for children," says one study.[36] Virtually no fruits or vegetables are advertised, while foods from the tip of the USDA food pyramid (fats and sweets) predominate.

I've seen a bumper sticker here and there that reads "Kill your TV." Is that supposed to be an ironic commentary on the link between TV and violent behavior? Whatever it means, I don't think the solution to the TV problem is quite that simple.

TV isn't inherently bad. It's how we use it that may be harmful to our mental and physical health. Hardly any parents I know haven't occasionally plugged in their kids on bad days or at stressful times, like when they're making dinner and their spouses aren't home yet. It's easy for any parent to use TV as a baby sitter, and it may be even more tempting for those who are with their children during days that can sometimes seem interminable. One mom who fervently believes in avoiding TV muses, "I didn't allow my kids to watch TV, but that also meant they were never away from me. Possibly it compromised my mental health because I never put a video in and walked away from them."

Computers Are Screens, Too

Many parents are also concerned about violence in video and computer games. But there are lots of educational games out there, too, right? And shouldn't we encourage kids to become technologically savvy to gain an edge in academics and the job market?

Not necessarily, say some experts. According to many parents, educators, and child development specialists, computer use can interfere with healthy development if it robs time from more active pursuits, isolates a child from family and friends, or reduces a child's ability to concentrate on a task or a text.[37] "Everything we know suggests that this technology may do more harm than good," says educational psychologist Jane Healy, author of the book *Failure to Connect,* in an article in *U.S. News and World Report.*[38] It may seem counterintuitive to limit children's access to computers in a society that can barely remember when a mouse was merely a rodent, but it's important to use computers in proportion to their true educational or entertainment value. A few hours per week of on-line research or high-quality software use may not be harmful—and may help a kid get comfortable with technology—but it's not going to get him or her into Harvard.

Tips for Using Screen Time Wisely

- *Set a time limit for your child.* My family's limit is a half-hour of screen time a day per child. The kids can use their time to play computer games, go on-line, or watch TV. We make exceptions for family movie nights, high-profile sports events like the Olympics, and programs on topics of special interest. If you like, you can track screen time with a simple chart. Get some stickers and assign a value to each. (Let's say each sticker represents a half-hour.) Each week give your child the appropriate number of stickers. Have your child put the stickers on a chart as screen time is spent. When the stickers are gone, no more screen time until next week.

- *Limit your own screen time.* Set a good example. I usually tape my two favorite TV shows so I can watch them after the kids are in bed and fast-forward through commercials. I use the computer only for

Screen It

For detailed descriptions of popular films with unbiased comments on issues of interest to parents, visit these web sites:

http://www.screenit.com

http://www.filmvalues.com/index.cfm

work, e-mail, and the occasional on-line purchase, so my kids aren't likely to find me aimlessly surfing the internet.

- *Establish priorities.* Homework, piano practice, and other responsibilities come before screen time in our house.

- *Critique commercials.* Discuss the purpose of commercials and how advertisers try to manipulate viewers' perceptions in order to sell their products.

- *Screen your child's selections.* Try to watch a program or movie before you let your child watch it so you can decide whether it's appropriate. Then discuss it with your child afterward. Always check out a computer game before you let your child use it. Ditto for web sites. Take advantage of any chat room screening devices or access restriction offered by your internet service provider. Don't assume that a movie, TV show, web site, or computer game approved by another parent will be okay with you; parents differ widely on what's acceptable for their kids. I'm more cautious than some parents I know and less cautious than others.

- *Control your screen population.* The fewer screens you have in your house, the less important they'll seem and the less they'll tempt you. You may want to have one computer and one TV, or perhaps just a computer and no TV. Figure out the minimum number of screens that would serve your family's needs.

Story Time: Encouraging Kids to Read and Listen

I bet that most kids, if they've either shaken or never developed a screen addiction, would rather read or be read to than spend time with a TV or computer. Reading, listening to, and talking about stories (and other literary forms) are perhaps the best ways to stimulate your child's intellect. These activities are also great fun for your child. They're engrossing and entertaining. They fuel your child's imagination, open his or her eyes to new worlds, and provide opportunities to spend time with you.

Reading has been a staple activity at our house since day one. Sharing stories from my childhood and discovering new ones with my children is one of my greatest parenting joys. My youngest is into Beverly Cleary's Ramona stories, which I loved as a child. My older daughter and I have just finished Louisa May Alcott's *Little Women*, another favorite of mine. My son and I have read the Chronicles of Narnia series by C. S. Lewis, which was new to me, together.

When you and your child read together, experiment with voices for different characters. Pronounce long words exquisitely. Get dramatic. If you don't enjoy reading aloud, get some story tapes from the library and listen to them together. Or attend your library's story hour. Or just make up stories! I tell my kids "Itty-Bitty Mouse" stories about a mouse family that lives in a house like ours. (Lots of parents make up stories about characters with names and traits remarkably similar to those of their own children.) Or listen to an old-fashioned radio show. My kids love Minnesota Public Radio's *A Prairie Home Companion* because of Garrison Keillor's superb storytelling, characters, and jokes.

Fifteen Ways to Promote Reading at Home

The following ideas are adapted from teacher educator Robert Morgan's "Creative Ways to Encourage Students to Read" at http://www.creativeteachingsite.com.

1. Read aloud to your child, regardless of his or her age. If an older child balks, just read newspaper articles aloud from time to time. Family read-aloud sessions are great for car trips and cold winter evenings.

2. If your child wants to read something to you, say yes…and be patient. Praise your child for his or her reading efforts.

3. Establish a family reading time. Let your child choose what to read. Don't force a reluctant reader; just knowing the time is reserved for reading is worthwhile.

4. Visit the library regularly, even if your child isn't interested in checking out books. Introduce your child to the librarians at your community and school libraries. Librarians are eager to help kids find interesting reading material.

5. Subscribe to a magazine for your child. The excitement of getting mail and the sense of ownership will make reading appealing.

6. Model reading. Children who see their parents reading often become readers and accept reading as a normal daily activity.

7. Display many and varied books prominently in your home—and set aside a place in your child's room for his or her books.

8. Recommend books to your child. Describe them a little and say how easy or hard they are. Let your child decide whether to read them.

9. If your child starts a book and doesn't want to finish it, accept that choice. (Hasn't that happened to you?)

10. When a topic involving the whole family arises—for example, an upcoming vacation—share books on it with the family.

11. Frequent places that sell books at low cost, like used book stores, library book sales, and garage sales.

12. Read the books your child reads and discuss them.

13. Discuss with your child ideas in the books *you* read.

14. When you and your child are working on a project with printed instructions, have your child read them aloud.

15. Check out text adventure games. (This is an old computer game genre that requires lots of reading and thinking. Entering *text adventure games* on any major internet search engine should yield many choices.)

Beyond the Home Zone

Though you may call yourself a stay-at-home parent, you certainly won't be home all the time! Taking your child out can salvage a crummy day or make an average day great. When you're home with your child on weekdays, you can schedule outings at the last minute and enjoy popular destinations when they're not crowded. Less waiting in lines for parking, admission, ice cream, and so on—it's just one more way at-home parenting relieves stress.

Action Spots: Parks and Playgrounds

Every kid needs to run, yell, climb, hang upside down, hunt for frogs, count ducks, and pretend to be a pirate, an astronaut, or an archaeologist. Find out where the best local parks and playgrounds are by asking friends or checking out a local parenting magazine. (Many publish "best of" lists that are sure to include favorite parks and playgrounds.)

We go in spurts; for a few weeks a certain park is our favorite, then we switch to another park. There's the park near the bakery where we can sample the bread and buy small cans of juice. There's the park near our house with the wading pool. There's the indoor park a few miles away, which is a great destination for cold days.

You get the idea. Pack a picnic and call some friends to meet you there!

Animals: Zoos and Nature Centers

Almost all kids love animals, and many zoos are designed with kids in mind. An annual membership is a great investment. If you pay the daily admission fee, you may feel you have to get your money's worth each time you visit. But if you have a membership that gives you unlimited admission, you can spend an hour watching the monkeys and leave knowing you'll get to the dolphins or the lions next time. If an annual membership is too pricey, consider doing what a friend of mine did: She bought a cheaper family pass at a zoo in a nearby city that offered reciprocal membership with our city's zoo.

A nature walk is many a child's first science lesson. Does your area have county or regional parks with hiking trails and interpretive centers? Many offer educational programs that give kids of various ages close-up and hands-on experiences with local flora and fauna, usually for a reasonable fee.

Art and Artifacts: Museums

If your town has an art, science, history, natural history, or children's museum, you may find an annual membership there worthwhile, too. If you're considering a membership, visit once before you sign up so you can find out whether your child is interested in what's offered or whether the atmosphere is kid-friendly. (If not, try again next year!) Some museums have free days or evenings so you can try before you buy.

Some spectacular art museums (such as New York's Museum of Modern Art on a busy Saturday, in my experience) maintain a stuffy, children-tolerated-but-not-entirely-welcome atmosphere, but many others try hard to attract their next generation of patrons. They offer kids' classes and family days focused on themes that appeal to children. My local art museum hands out brochures kids can use to hunt for specific images throughout the galleries.

Science, history, and children's museums usually have lots of hands-on exhibits for kids to delve into. A natural history museum is a logical destination for little ones, too. What could be more fascinating than room after room of dinosaur skeletons, exotic stuffed animals, and life-size or miniature dioramas of people from other times and places? You can read the plaques on the walls while your child oohs and aahs over the exhibits.

ABCs: Public Libraries

It's hard to beat the library as a kid-friendly destination. Most modern libraries have children's sections that offer story hours for preschoolers, toddler areas with board books and toys, comfy seating, fish tanks, kid-size tables and chairs, and shelves and shelves of picture books, chapter books, beloved series, videotapes, and CDs. And best of all, libraries are still free.

Beating the Back-Seat Blues

Researchers from the U.S. Department of Transportation say that children ages five and younger today spend an average of sixty-five minutes a day riding around in cars, and children ages six to eighteen spend sixty-one minutes a day in cars (excluding time spent on a school bus).[39] Many at-home parents log even longer hours—particularly if they have older children, whose schedules may include sports practices, music lessons, religious education, sleepovers, and more. Pity the toddler in tow.

Sedentary time in the car means less time for play and exercise—which isn't helpful for kids growing up in a culture that's already putting them at risk for obesity by promoting junk food and passive entertainment. One mom notes that when her family lived in London and walked or took public transportation everywhere, her children seemed trimmer and more energetic.[40] But let's face it: You're going to have to tote your child around at least some of the time. Here are some ideas to minimize the negative effects of too many miles behind the wheel and in the back seat:

- Play word games or simply talk with your child. If your child spends much of the day in school, the car can be a great place to catch up on events or get your child to open up. I ended up having "the talk" (about where babies come from) unexpectedly in the car one day.

- Listen to books on tape or good music. Expand your listening horizons: Try the classical station if you're sick of hearing your favorite band touted as classic rock or check out the country station during public radio pledge week.

- Make sure your child is safely restrained. Read the instructions for your car seat or booster seat—and follow them! I was in an accident once with my toddler and preschooler along. My car was totaled, but my kids, safely strapped in, were fine. I never grumbled about using car seats again.

- Leave your child at home occasionally. One at-home mom who lives near Washington D.C. says she's hired a baby sitter two days a week to minimize the time her two-year-old spends in the car while she ferries her older kids around in infamous beltway traffic.

- As tempting as it may be (especially if your child is asleep), never leave your child unattended in a car, even for a few minutes. It's not only against the law in many states, it's also dangerous. Excessive heat or cold, an unexpected delay, or an unsavory passerby could harm your child.

- Walk, bike, or ride the bus when you can instead of driving. Make getting there part of the fun!

Roulette Days

You're bound to have days when routine turns into roulette and you have no idea where you're going to land. At any moment, something unexpected—an invitation you can't pass up (or one you wish you could); a car, computer, or furnace breakdown; a sick child or pet (or worse yet, a sick you)—can make a mess of your tidy schedule. Here are a few strategies for surviving roulette days:

- Focus on the big picture. Remember how much you love your kids and your partner.

- Ask for help. Call a friend or neighbor to give you a lift, lend you a car, or watch your child for a half-hour.

- Be kind to yourself. This is no time to think about your master's thesis or fitting into your size-eight jeans.

- Go with the flow. Take deep breaths. Eat chocolate. Leave the grocery cart in the aisle and go home if the kids are screaming. Take a walk instead of a nap or a nap instead of a walk.

Routine, Not Roulette

Life with a child can be chaotic. To help your household run as smoothly as possible, invest some time and effort in establishing routines. You'll be glad you did!

Routines not only create a calmer, safer home, they also help children develop self-control; independence; responsibility; adaptability; decision-making, problem-solving, and memory skills; respect for others and for rules and limits; and appreciation of both order and flexibility. And last but by no means least, routines can help parents get regular doses of much-needed downtime.

Stay-at-home parents have an advantage in establishing routines because the more time kids spend with their parents, the more exposure to family routines they get. As a result, they may learn and accept these routines more easily.

The trick to winning this kind of roulette is letting go of your agenda and congratulating yourself on learning an important parenting lesson: You're not really in control anymore.

Infant Routines

For many parents, the most chaotic time is baby's first year, when they're adjusting to interrupted sleep, learning to interpret crying, and struggling to maintain their identities as their lives are changed forever by a small, weak stranger with an iron grip on their hearts. But even parents of infants can recognize daily patterns and begin to establish routines.

Newborns spend most of their time sleeping and eating, so newborn routines revolve around these activities. For the first few months a baby dictates the timing, but parents can dictate the other details. Here are a few tips for establishing consistency with infants:

- Sit in the same place for every feeding if possible.
- Keep the feeding area lit so your baby doesn't doze off.
- Create a simple ritual to help your baby recognize when it's time to sleep. For example, you might feed your baby, change his or her diaper, sing a lullaby, then put your baby to bed.
- Take note of your baby's natural tendencies and act accordingly. For example, if water stimulates your baby, don't plan a bath right before bedtime.
- Put your baby to bed while he or she is still awake so your baby learns how to fall asleep without help.
- Play with your baby when he or she is in a quiet, alert mood, not a sleepy or fussy one.
- Take at least fifteen minutes twice a day for yourself while your baby is sleeping or being cared for by someone else. Use the time to read, relax, sleep, exercise, or do whatever recharges your batteries.

As your baby grows older, you can establish more routines and exert more control over timing.

Routines for Older Kids

Parents of older kids may find it helpful to establish routines for all recurring activities, such as meals, bedtime, play time, homework, chores, and special events like sleepovers. Well-established routines are often viewed as procedures rather than rules and can keep nagging and arguing to a minimum. Here are some tips to help you build and maintain routines with your older child:

- Explain why a particular routine is needed.
- When a routine is started, give ample warnings and frequent reminders. Later, keep them short and use them sparingly to

prevent arguments and avoid nagging. Written reminders posted in appropriate places may be helpful.

- Tune in to your child's personality. For example, if your school-age child isn't a morning person, an evening routine might include packing his or her backpack and choosing clothes for the next day.

- Tie routines to other actions or occurrences. For example, you might say, "When you dry your hands, wipe up splashes with the hand towel before you hang it up" or, "When you hear mommy come home from work, it's time to put your toys away and wash up for supper."

- Establish a routine with a concrete action of your own. For example, give your child an alarm clock and explain that you've set it for the time you'd like him or her to get out of bed in the morning.

- Perform routines together. For example, brush your teeth together.

- If a routine involves time, allow more time than an adult would need to complete it. This can prevent rushing, which in turn can prevent anxiety and resentment.

- Once you establish a routine, stick to it.

- Discuss when and why a routine might change. For example, you might consider a later bedtime when your child turns ten. Or when you have a special visitor, you might postpone your child's household chores until after the visitor leaves.

- If your child wants to renegotiate a routine, stick to the routine for now but agree to discuss it at a specific time in the future.

The Importance of Nap Time and Bedtime

Establishing sleeping patterns is one of the first and best ways families can gain a sense of orderly life. Helping children get the proper amount of sleep for their age and temperament is important for everyone.

When Kids Snooze, You Can't Lose

Most infants take two or more naps a day, often adjusting to a single daily nap by age one or one-and-a-half. As they near kindergarten, most children give up daily naps. Some five-year-olds continue to nap a few times a week.

As a stay-at-home parent, you'll find that regular naps are as valuable as gold—not only because they help your child avoid the unpleasant behavior characteristic of tired children, but also because they give *you* a break. Whether you grab a cup of coffee and a book, make a few phone calls, fold laundry, put dishes away, or catch some z's yourself, you'll both be refreshed when your child wakes up. You might think napping would make kids stay up later at night, but surprisingly, many children sleep better at night if they get a nap during the day. Also, establishing a firm nap schedule early on can help children maintain a habit of daily quiet time when they eventually outgrow naps—whether they're two or twelve.

Getting into the Nap Habit

When my two older children were small, a regular nap routine helped me stay sane and feel organized and purposeful, so I made it a priority. Our system went something like this:

1. After lunch, I cleared the table and battened down the hatches.

2. With my baby daughter in my arms, I ushered my three-year-old son to his bedroom and instructed him to read or play quietly until I'd put his sister down for her nap.

3. I read a quick story to the baby, then rocked and cuddled her a bit. I laid her in her crib with board books and sang while rubbing her tummy.

4. I smiled, said, "See you in a little while," left her room, and closed the door.

5. I went to my son's room, and we read stories in his bed until he (or often we) fell asleep.

Nap time with my youngest child was bliss. I had her all to myself many afternoons while the older kids were playing elsewhere or at school, and we two would curl up together and nap in my room. By then I'd abandoned my "shoulds" about productivity during nap time. Instead, I embraced it as a form of self-care. I was working hard raising three kids, and if a break during the day refreshed me, then that's what I needed to do.

Maybe I just lucked out and ended up with kids willing to conform to a nap routine. But I like to think that because I made nap time manda- tory—and shaped it as a time for bonding with stories, songs, and rit- ual—it became a welcome part of their day. Their sleep personalities, formed in those early years, show themselves even now: I think my son, now twelve, would still nap after lunch if he could! He's the kind of kid who's out as soon as his head hits the pillow. My older daughter, however, is a night owl—often found reading in bed and almost always the last child to fall asleep at night.

Quiet Time as an Alternative

If your child is not a napper, establish quiet time, during which everyone in the house is expected to read, rest, or do some quiet indoor activity. A half-hour is probably reasonable, but experiment with more time and see how it goes. Set a timer to enforce the sanctity of quiet time. Making the timer the enforcer rather than mom or dad prevents power struggles.

Good Night Moon

Evening bedtime routines are every bit as important as daytime nap rituals. Some parents let their kids stay up until they go to bed to maximize family time. Others set a kids' bedtime that permits an hour or two of adult time in the evening. Here are a few tried and true bedtime tips:

- Keep in mind that while it's your responsibility to get your child to bed, falling asleep is your child's responsibility—regardless of his or her age.

- Some parents find a pacifier useful in helping a baby get to sleep without nursing or a bottle. To avoid dependence on pacifiers, you can limit their use to bedtime and nap time.

- Allow your child transition time. Give a ten-minute warning and set a timer to announce when bedtime has arrived.

- Help your child calm down mentally and physically with a hygiene routine, a bedtime chat, and/or a story. Limit the number of bedtime stories or songs to prevent stalling.

- Taking a comfort object like a special blanket or doll to bed can help a child feel secure. (Don't put a large, soft stuffed animal or blanket in an infant's crib, as such items can inhibit breathing.) A night-light might also do the trick.

- If your child tends to get out of bed after you leave the room, send him or her back to bed and say you'll check up in five minutes. Then check on your child before he or she has a chance to pop out of bed again.

In families with a stay-at-home parent, bedtime duties often fall on the parent not at home during the day. But if both parents can be involved, bedtime often goes more smoothly and quickly. With one child, for example, one parent could give a bath, then the other could read a story and tuck the child in bed. With two kids, each parent could put one child to bed. With more, it's either a group good night—the kids all get herded to bed simultaneously—or a round robin, with parents visiting each one separately for a good-night kiss, a last drink of water, or a brief chat.

Changing Needs

Your child's sleep needs will change. For example, as children get older, they may take fewer naps and want more activity. Children in school may need to go to bed earlier. As an at-home parent, you have ample opportunity to watch your child's needs and preferences emerge and change. You can adjust family routines to meet your child's needs or gently nudge your child toward a routine that works for the family.

For example, if your child leads a very busy life during the school year, during the summer you may want to set a later bedtime (especially if it's still light outside) and let him or her sleep in to provide more rest and unstructured play. Or if your preschooler likes to take an hour-long afternoon nap at two o'clock, but you need to pick up your first-grader at three, you could change your preschooler's afternoon routine over a couple of weeks. You might serve lunch a few minutes

Adjusted Expectations

Jeanne, the mother of two children under age three, has adjusted both her family's routines and her own expectations to meet everyone's needs as best she can.

She made a slow transition from working full-time as the director of a human services planning agency to being at home full-time. She's still involved in the public sphere as a volunteer on several neighborhood and city planning committees. She's also committed to keeping a journal of her children's activities and sending daily updates to both sets of grandparents, who live far away.

"I need spare time for lots of things. Squeezing it all in is hard!" Jeanne says. But, "I like to contribute to the community. I'd hate to give it up, to lose the connections."

Jeanne does her phone and computer work while her kids nap. Nap time is late in the afternoon, from four to six o'clock. Her husband comes home at six and takes over caring for the children while she takes some time for herself and prepares dinner. Everyone turns in for the night at the same time—about eleven o'clock.

The children don't always nap simultaneously, but Jeanne takes a glass-half-full view of her situation. She says even a half-hour of kid-free time in the afternoon helps her feel relaxed and productive. She'd prefer an hour—or even better, two hours—but she'll settle for less. She explains, "It only takes one good day [when both kids nap together] to make my week! My expectations are lower."

Real-Life Rituals

- I take my younger daughter to the same coffee shop every Wednesday morning for a glazed donut while her siblings go to school choir practice.

- A group of families whose daughters are on the same swim team go out for pizza together on Friday evenings after practice.

- One family vacations at the same Bermuda resort every year. They're not wealthy, but everyone in the family enjoys this annual ritual so much that they budget for it.

- Every year my family and I go to Christmas Eve mass, have a party at our house afterward, and spend Christmas morning around our tree. My kids know exactly what to expect and look forward to helping with the preparations.

- Another family participates in the yearly May Day parade in our community. They work for weeks in advance to create their roles and costumes. Mom calls this event her family's "high holy days."

- One at-home mom rattles off several simple rituals her family practices, such as taking annual weekend camping trips, having ice cream at a coffee shop after school conferences, using a "blessing cup" for special days, and eating Pop-Tarts on vacation.

earlier each day or allow a few extra minutes outdoors after lunch so your child is ready for a nap at one-thirty. You're still honoring the need for an afternoon nap while adjusting the routine to work for everyone.

From Routines to Rituals

The routines that young children need often change as they grow older. They become more experienced, more able, and more independent, and as a result, they usually want more freedom to choose how they spend their time and whom they spend it with. But even as kids grow older, routines—whether they're daily, weekly, seasonal, or annual—can continue to contribute to a family's emotional health. As one stay-at-home mom points out, they're positive reminders of what makes each family unique.

William Doherty is the director of the marriage and family therapy program at the University of Minnesota. In his book *The Intentional Family*, Doherty explains that family rituals create the time and emotional space for parent-child communication to grow. He believes that families who create and maintain family rituals stand a better chance of weathering the storms of peer pressure and popular culture.

Doherty defines a family ritual as any act or event that's repeated, coordinated, and meaningful: for example, eating dinner at home together every night or celebrating a particular holiday the same way each year. In addition to rituals that involve the whole family, parents who have multiple kids can also establish a ritual with each child, such as shooting baskets on Sunday mornings or walking the dog together after dinner. Rituals need not be expensive, nor must they be tied to special events like vacations or holidays (though these events do lend themselves to rituals).

Arlene R. Cardozo, author of the book *Sequencing*, which presents her personal experience and her research on the trend of women leaving the work force temporarily to stay home with children, writes that her grown daughters say their happiest early memories are of the mealtime rituals she established with them. One daughter fondly recalls a picnic spot they frequented; another says she enjoyed eating lunch together at a particular table. It's not the well-planned birthday parties, school plays, or holidays that these women remember; it's the small, everyday activities they did with their parents.

Discipline: Teaching Self-Control

Every child must learn to follow rules. Every family, playground, school, or team sets expectations about appropriate behavior and enforces consequences for inappropriate behavior. For example, a family may have rules limiting how far a child can go from the front yard, forbidding certain swearing and name-calling, setting curfews for teens, and determining whether a child can visit a friend's house if the friend's parents aren't home.

Tolerance for rule-breaking varies, but most healthy families respond with some sort of consequence when kids step out of bounds. A classic consequence is the time-out: A child who hits or calls names, for example, might be asked to separate from others for a short time to think about his or her behavior and consider better ways to handle his or her feelings. A time-out may be followed by a brief discussion with mom or dad to discuss the child's findings. Other examples: Using a forbidden word requires the offender to put money in a "swear jar," the contents of which are later donated to charity. An older child who breaks rules might have to forego a privilege next time around. For example, staying out past curfew could mean no Friday night movie with friends next weekend. It's helpful to remind children that when adults fail to follow rules, they experience consequences, too, such as paying fines to a library or video store for late returns or to the city for not putting money in parking meters. Parents can

Five Ways to Cool Your Jets

When you feel your temper about to boil over, turn down the heat with one of these tips:

- *Count to ten.* Add a few deep breaths if you're really on edge.
- *Let off some steam.* If your child's loudness, fidgeting, or arguing is grating on your nerves, shout, "Run around the house three times!" or, "Do twenty jumping jacks!" A quick shout lets you vent your frustration without getting angry, and the physical activity lets your child burn off extra energy harmlessly.
- *Remember that your child's agenda differs from yours.* A toddler who has no sense of time, for example, won't understand why you're in a hurry to get to the bank before it closes.
- *Whisper.* When you feel like yelling, do the opposite: Lower your voice and speak as calmly as you can. Remember that old ad slogan *If you want to get someone's attention, whisper?* It works. Sometimes, anyway.
- *Give yourself a time-out.* Tell your child why you're doing it: You're so angry or frustrated or tired right now that you need to be quiet and think about how to act.

also explain that rules are meant to help people live together safely and pleasantly.

Effective discipline is not a matter of exerting external control; after all, it's impossible to control another person. Rather, it's a matter of teaching self-control.[41] I think our society underestimates the innate capacity of children to exercise self-control. Children are capable of sustained concentration, quiet, and respectful treatment of others, but adults sometimes don't give them enough opportunities to use these skills. If we let TV put kids in a trance, give them poor nutrition, or completely program their lives for them, they may develop weak imagination or social skills, may be physically incapable of appropriate behavior, or may be unable to decide how to spend their time. In other words, we should expect kids to respond to the opportunities and guidance (or lack thereof) we give them.

Mellowing Yelling

Yelling is a natural response to misbehavior—especially continued misbehavior—but it's also counterproductive.[42] Some yelling is probably inevitable, but many parents believe it's a good idea to keep it to a minimum.

One mother points out that it's easy to revert to yelling when you're stressed out—especially if you were raised in a family in which yelling was acceptable. "I use yelling as my barometer," she says. "When I'm yelling, I [know I] need to take better care of myself. That's not the kind of parent I want to be." When she feels anger rising, she tries to get everyone out of the house or change courses with one of her favorite activities, reading aloud.

Preventing Power Struggles

In 1964 child psychiatrist Rudolf Dreikurs wrote a classic book on child rearing called *Children: The Challenge.* I read it while working at a daycare center several years before I became a parent, and its message stuck with me.

Dreikurs suggests that parents can help their children develop self-discipline without exhausting, stressful power struggles. The discipline methods he advocates are based on this idea: Children should learn from experience that their actions have logical consequences.

For example, if a child refuses to wear a jacket in cold weather, he or she is bound to get chilly at the playground or be kept indoors at recess. By experiencing the consequence of this choice, the child learns there's a good reason to wear a jacket in cold weather; it's not just a parental whim. Or suppose a child wants to go to a movie with a friend but can't because his or her allowance for the week has already been spent on candy. In the future, the child will learn to plan ahead and budget.

Dreikurs's methods prevent typical parent-child power struggles by offering the child choices and relieving the parent of the role of villain or killjoy. Every day brings many opportunities to practice these methods: "Would you like to have peanut butter

Pick Your Battles

Martha worked with developmentally disabled and mentally ill adults before she became a mom. "That job really prepared me for mothering," she says, laughing. "One thing I learned is that some people go looking for a power struggle! They want to feel power," she says. "If we just let them, it solves so many problems."

Martha says another important lesson she learned is that "your first reaction is not always your best one." It's easy to get sucked into a fight with a child who's challenging your authority, but engaging in a battle of wills with a three-year-old, she suggests, is counterproductive. She advises parents to watch for thoughts like *I'm not going to take it anymore* or *I'm going to put my foot down,* which may signal the beginning of a power struggle. If you find yourself getting locked in a power struggle with your kids, Martha says, "Ask yourself, 'Does it really matter?'"

HALT at the Heart of the Problem

Suzanne, an at-home mother of three, offers this quick assessment tool: "I use the buzzword *HALT*. If my kids aren't coping well, or they're fighting, I ask myself, 'Are they *h*ungry, *a*ngry, *l*onely, or *t*ired?'" She stops for a moment to figure out if the problem is caused by one of these common factors, then tries to meet the unmet need and restore harmony.

and jelly or grilled cheese?" "Would you like to walk or ride in the stroller?" Such choices give children some control over their daily lives—a bit of the power they crave. And because these choices limit a child's responses, they help parents manage the hundreds of daily tasks and decisions that are part of living with children.

Parents must, however, be prepared to live with their children's choices. For example, if your child decides to walk and then grows tired, you may need to remind your child that he or she chose to walk. You may endure some tears as your child learns to accept consequences, but your child will learn from experience and hopefully build on that experience to make good choices in the future.

Coping with Crying

Hush, Little Baby

Dealing with crying (baby's, not yours—we'll talk about that in the next chapter) is a huge parenting challenge. A baby's crying is one of the most stressful sounds a parent can hear. Certain kinds of distressed infant crying actually trigger a hormonal response in both men and women, according to Sarah Blaffer Hrdy in her book *Mother Nature*.[43] To this day, a certain kind of crying makes me feel anxious—and then relieved when I realize it's not my child who's crying.

The inconsolable crying of an infant with colic is perhaps the most nerve-wracking kind because its cause is still not fully understood, and there isn't much to do but ride it out for weeks or months until the colic subsides. Some parents benefit from strategies like changing their diets if they're nursing (dairy products, beans, onions, or other foods may contribute to a baby's discomfort), holding their babies in different positions, taking their babies for car rides, and putting their babies in car seats on top of clothes dryers (the vibrations may soothe a baby). But perhaps the two most useful tools for coping with colic are patience and periodic breaks from the baby. Rebecca, a single mother of two teens, says of her colicky first-born, "I had to hand him to someone else to hold sometimes...so I could look at him and see how beautiful he was."

Babies must be so frustrated when hunger, pain, discomfort, loneliness, or any number of other feelings well up—and they have no way to communicate their needs and wants. Imagine being in a land where everyone is bigger and more powerful than you and you rely on others to meet all your needs. The giants all emit sounds, but you can't make sense of them at first. Even when you start to understand the sound patterns, you can't make the sounds yourself. Your options are to be compliant and winning in order to stay in the giants' favor or to let go with all your might so they'll come running. Well, what would you do?

At-home parents may endure more crying than parents working outside the home simply because they spend more time with their children. But this cloud does have a silver lining: With more exposure to crying, at-home parents may learn more quickly how to interpret their babies' different cries. This helps them respond appropriately to meet their children's needs and reduce the overall amount of distress their children—and in turn, they—suffer.

Dealing with an Older Child's Distress

If you learn to recognize behavior patterns and anticipate your child's needs, you may be able to see storm clouds forming and disperse them before tears begin to fall. For example, you may figure out that when your child's whine starts escalating, he or she is fixing to throw a fit. Or perhaps you notice that your child gets fussy every day around three o'clock. (You can set your watch by some children's mood swings.) To prevent tears, you might offer a snack or tuck your child in for a nap.

Of course, sometimes you just can't predict or explain a child's crying. If your child cries or exhibits distress for no apparent reason, assume there is a reason even if you can't see or understand it. Help your child calm down as best you can—which usually means just being there, offering a lap or a long hug.

The best response to a temper tantrum (an outburst of passionate crying, screaming, and/or physical rage) is ignoring it. If you can outlast a good old-fashioned fit by simply removing yourself as an audience, your child will realize that tantrums are useless and will try a different—hopefully more civil—way to communicate next time. If your child has three or more temper tantrums per day, seek professional help to rule out a medical or psychological cause.

To handle crying prompted by another child's behavior, taunts, or exclusion or some other real or perceived injustice or injury, first remain calm yourself. Gently distract your child and just be there to hold him or her if desired. Breathe deeply. If your child is old enough to talk, listen to the problem and affirm—don't try to solve—it. Say things like "Yes, I can tell you are angry," "You sound very sad," or, "Would you like to tell me about that?" Let your child feel his or her emotions and don't try to diminish them or provide all the answers.

A couple of summers ago my younger daughter was trying hard to learn to ride a two-wheeler. She often asked her dad to take her out riding as she valiantly tried to balance without training wheels. She came home in tears one night because he'd tried letting go of her bike, and she'd fallen. As she walked into the house sobbing, I could tell she needed to vent her frustration. She needed me to listen to her feelings, not make them go away. I took her in my arms and said, "I know it hurts. You really want to ride that bike and you're working very hard." I reminded her that most people fall when they're just learning to ride. She still felt sad, but she knew her feelings were acknowledged and respected.

They Grow Up So Fast

If you've got a small child, you've undoubtedly heard some experienced parent or grandparent say wistfully, "They grow up so fast," and thought, "Yeah, right. I'm counting down the minutes until bedtime." Ah, we've all been there. Here's a saying I've heard a few times that describes this parenting paradox: *When your kids are little, the hours seem like days. When they grow up, the days seem like hours.*

It's a bittersweet thing, watching my kids grow up. I miss the feeling that I'm indispensable to them—only I can breastfeed them, only I can accurately interpret their two-year-old speech, only I know exactly how to read *Goodnight Moon.* At the same time, I think their growth is wonderful. We can take half-day bike rides; compare notes about *Star Trek*; play long, spirited rounds of Uno, Sorry!, and Monopoly; and tell jokes that don't start with "knock knock." We've just discovered the fun of three-on-two basketball games in the back yard. I'm beginning to see hints of the adults my kids will become and to reap the rewards of all the hard work I did to entertain and sustain them during the physically intense early years.

But I know my kids' growth doesn't mean they need me any less. Let's face it: they need me to drive them everywhere! Many parents of school-age children feel as if they're spending their lives in their cars. But there are lots of other important ways at-home parents can help older kids.

Helping Kids Face the Challenges of Growing Up

As children grow older, their questions get harder—not easier—to answer: *Why is the sky blue?* is a piece of cake compared to *Where do babies come from?* or *Did you ever drink/smoke/cheat/lie/have sex/do drugs?*

For many children the elementary school years are smooth sailing, because children at this age (approximately six to twelve) tend to be less inwardly focused than preschoolers and teenagers and more interested in learning about their world. Still, many children in this age group face challenges involving friendships, popularity, responsibility, and social issues. They may feel left out of birthday parties or recess games or feel conflicted by allegiances to competing groups or activities. Toward the end of this stage, kids may experience the onset of puberty and become more aware of their developing sexuality. They may also become more concerned about current events; for example, my twelve-year-old pays close attention to media coverage of unrest in the Middle East and local, national, and international efforts at peacemaking. Parents can best serve their children during these years by staying aware of what their children are thinking and feeling.

Thoughts from the Teen Trenches

"Today's junior high kids are exposed to things we weren't exposed to until we were seventeen or eighteen," says Suzanne, mother of three girls (the oldest in seventh grade). She's referring to drugs, alcohol, and sexual knowledge and activity. She believes that being an at-home parent helps her stay closely involved in her children's lives and shape their experiences in a positive way. "It means volunteering in school, being home when they get home, being aware of what's going into their brains, screening things," she says. She and her husband hope their daughters grow up with "the tools to be law-abiding, respectful people of integrity. Those qualities really need to be built at home."

A well-known public service announcement says, "If you want to know what your kids are thinking, ask them." I'd add, "Expect answers—don't settle for 'I dunno' or 'Fine.'" Here are a few tips to help you conduct a gentle inquiry without sounding like the FBI:

- Ask open-ended questions.
- Pose the same question a few different ways.
- Keep a sense of humor.
- If your child seems sad or frustrated, help him or her find words to express these feelings.
- Use car-pooling duty to eavesdrop on what kids are really talking about, since they tend to forget you're there.

If your child wants help with a particular problem, be willing to brainstorm solutions and let your child pick the one he or she likes best. For example, if your child is being excluded from soccer games at recess, you could say, "I can think of three things you could do. What do *you* think some options are?" Chances are your child will come up with at least one of the options on your list, which might include finding a trusted person in the game and asking to join, requesting an adult's help, or finding another group of kids to play with. Even if your ideas don't work like magic, just providing them will tell your child that he or she has an ally in you.

The challenges and dangers that confront children as they navigate adolescence and the teen years make this a tough time for everyone. You can probably recall pretty vividly your own journey through this rocky phase. It hasn't gotten easier; in fact, the life of an adolescent may be more difficult and risky than ever. An older child searching for his or her identity in a challenging world needs the security of parental love and presence just as much as a toddler venturing away from mom or dad for the first time. Many parents say the key is to simply be there and be ready to listen at the "drop everything" moment when a child is open to revealing what's on his or her mind.

Mary Dee explains the benefits of being home with her two preteens: "I'm able to spend more time with the kids, to set the tone, to do triage," which she explains as deciding when and how to intervene and redirect her early adolescent children as they respond to the natural social pull of their peers. "I can exert more influence over them."

Mary, the mother of three children in high school or close to it, has seen a few of her friends' children go through crises of chemical abuse, serious depression, and running away from home. She wonders, "Will [my kids] be mentally healthy and in a good place when they're sixteen? I think it's really important for me to be home for them to make sure they're doing safe things."

The developmental task of any child is to push toward independence. And the older children get, the more pressure they feel from peers and popular culture. Today's adolescents and teens have to cope with not only the inevitable hormonal changes that affect their self-image and identity, but also decisions about dating, sexual activity, drugs, alcohol, driving, and so on. The after-school hours, when many teens are home alone, are said to be windows of opportunity for experimenting with sex and drugs. Parents who arrange their schedules to be home when their kids are believe they can thwart negative peer influences—and prevent negative consequences—of teens having too much unsupervised, unstructured time. There are other ways to keep tabs on kids, too: Don't be afraid to call another child's parents to verify that they'll be home if your child is planning to spend time there. Better yet, get to know the parents of your child's friends and see where your values mesh and diverge.

Finally, don't be afraid to set boundaries. Kids really do want them, even if they act sullen or defiant about them. Some parents suggest setting specific start and end times even for casual gatherings of friends—say, from five to nine o'clock. Such a time frame allows kids ample time to have fun without wearing out their welcome or feeling pressure to move outside their comfort zones. You might also give your child a few stock excuses to help him or her get out of an uncomfortable situation: "My mom will kill me if she smells smoke on my clothes!" or "I have to be home by eleven, or my parents won't let me use the car again." One mom says, "I tell my kids, 'Blame me!'" Teens should also know that no matter where they are, they can call their parents for a ride home if they're feeling uneasy.

Looking Back and Looking Ahead

I remember realizing with amazement when my oldest turned ten that I'd been doing the incredibly challenging, hands-on, head-intensive, emotionally draining, joyful work of mothering twenty-four hours a day, seven days a week, for a whole decade! That was certainly longer than I'd done any other job—or had even lived in the same place—since childhood. I felt very proud of all I'd accomplished and learned.

I remember, too, the first weeks of motherhood with my first-born. In the shelter of the maternity ward, surrounded by family, friends, doctors, and nurses, I was never alone. After a couple of days I emerged from that cocoon to head home with my husband and newborn son. On the short drive from the hospital to my house, all the familiar buildings and roads—even my own street and my own house—seemed transformed because of the new baby I had with me. Eventually the hoopla died down, the visitors stopped descending, the phone didn't ring as often, and I started feeling quite alone. I wished I'd had a road map to guide me in my new life as a parent.

No matter how much time you've spent as a parent, you're bound to feel occasionally that you've made some mistakes. That's natural, say the grandparents I know. But when all is said and done—and parenting, say the same grandparents, is never done!—most parents reassure themselves that they've done the best they could.

There is no road map. The road is made by walking. The best way to approach this lifelong journey is to make sure you have some traveling companions to provide the support you'll need—and that's the subject of the next chapter, Caring for You.

Chapter 4

Caring for You

The Emotional Costs of Your Choice

The Conversation Stopper

Just about every at-home parent I've ever talked to has some version of this story: You're at a party, and someone asks, "So, what do *you* do?" You answer, "I'm a stay-at-home mom (or dad)." Conversation screeches to a halt, and you're guaranteed one of two responses. The person either turns away without another word or practically pats you on the head with a patronizing reply.

"Oh, you must be *so* busy!" the person gushes. You want to scream, "You have no idea!" Or the person says, "Good for you. I could *never* do that," as if you clean toilets with a toothbrush for a living. Or you're branded as an "earth mother," which is how I once overheard a well-paid professional mom dismissively describe at-home moms. Or the person suddenly sees you as an ambitionless throwback, a loser mooching off your partner—though he or she won't tell you this to your face.

Counting the Cost

Everything from what you wear to where you lunch changes radically when you decide to

It Ain't Easy

"It's monotonous being with kids. They need routine, consistency, predictability. It's not the stuff great novels are written about!"
—*Cary, at-home mom of two*

"I think staying home is great for the kids, but not for the mom."
—*Kim, former at-home mom of two*

"Before [one of my husband's] shows opened, there would be a week when he just wasn't around. I'd be alone... the baby would get sick...I felt jealous, tired. I was still close to the theater at that time. Somehow I'd manage to go to the opening night, and I'd feel fat (or in my mind I was), and here were all these people I knew clicking with one another and being snazzy. They'd ask me, 'So what are you doing now?' I felt a peer pressure that would emotionally wreck me for a few days."
—*Nanci, at-home mom of three and erstwhile actor*

be an at-home parent. The persona you've built through years of daily work outside the home can evaporate faster than ammonia from a diaper pail. "I feel a little countercultural," says one at-home father, "not because I'm a stay-at-home dad, but because we have a stay-at-home parent at all. Sometimes I feel I'm on the outside looking in."

Emotionally speaking, it costs a lot to be a good parent. Putting your wants and sometimes even your basic needs on hold is par for the course. If you're a stay-at-home parent, you've probably given up a job and a paycheck. You may not be using many of your nonparental skills and talents. And no matter how much you like being home with your child or how secure you are in your choice, you're bound to feel one or more of the following:

- A deep sense of *loss* of your preparent identity
- *Isolation* from other adults
- *Exhaustion* due to the incessant physical and mental demands made of you as a caregiver, especially by infants and young children
- *Boredom* with the repetition of a home-centered daily life

Still, you may find yourself thinking the same words spoken by one at-home mom of three kids ages six and younger: "Just because it's hard doesn't mean I shouldn't be doing it!" If you're determined to "do it" despite the common frustrations, you must learn how to cope with them. Looking them full in the face is the first step.

Acknowledging Your Needs

Beyond the Mother-Martyr

How a woman perceives the role of mother depends on what she's learned about it from her social experiences, her culture and/or religion, and most importantly, her mother. A woman immersed since childhood in traditional gender expectations and icons of motherhood may not even realize that mothers have needs. Such a woman may have a hard time letting go of the mother-martyr myth—the concept that an ideal mother takes care of everyone else first. And since staying home may be considered a privilege, some women feel guilty if they don't enjoy every minute of it, if they need to ask for help, or if they present a less than impeccable image to the outside world.

However an at-home mom views her role, it's crucial that she realize she *does* have needs. Her situation is challenging, and if she doesn't take the time or make the effort to care for herself, she'll have a hard time meeting those challenges.

A new mother, for example, must cope with the biological realities of pregnancy and childbirth. Her body is in flux from conception through approximately the first year of her child's life. Pregnancy and childbirth put tremendous stress on her body. Her hormones fluctuate dramatically during pregnancy and breastfeeding. Her body continually changes size and shape. If she's nursing, her body is literally at her baby's beck and call.

A new mom faces many emotional challenges, too. She may not be pleased with the changes in her appearance and may struggle to find time for self-care. If she's shifting from employment to stay-at-home parenting, she may wrestle with her self-image. Before she stayed home, she probably felt competent in her work, compensated by her salary, and gratified to make an impact in her field, work with peers, and use her creativity and intellect. In her new role, she's starting from scratch. She must learn to care for the brand-new person she's brought into the world. She probably has intense feelings for her baby and high expectations of herself as she strives to meet her baby's needs. She may also find the lion's share of household responsibilities falling in her lap.

Cary recalls grappling with these questions when she was a new mom: *How do I get time for myself? Is it okay to want that if you're a mom at home?* She says it was a huge emotional struggle to give herself permission to take time away from her baby.

The Paternal Instinct

Maybe at-home moms should swipe a page from the at-home dad's playbook. Dads seem to be less stuck on the shoulds and more tuned in to the coulds when it comes to caregiving and household management. How do they do it?

Though a man's world is certainly changed forever when he becomes a father, there's a lot less emotional and cultural baggage about what makes an "ideal" dad than there is about moms. Sadly, North American society seems to be grateful to dads for *any* involvement in child rearing. We don't assume there's a "paternal instinct" comparable to the "maternal instinct" we hear so much about. Also, a father's mental

Dads' Needs

Paul, an electrical engineer on leave from his job at a large corporation, took his baby daughter on rounds to "every lumberyard in town." While the baby napped, he worked on a basement remodeling project. He says the project gave him personal satisfaction and a sense of accomplishment that he didn't get from the daily duties of diaper changing and bottle washing.

Robert practiced social work part-time and wrote a book during some of his twelve years at home as his children's primary caregiver. He now teaches psychology at Oakton Community College in Des Plaines, Illinois. He encourages all at-home parents to pursue an outside interest, whether it's part-time work, a hobby, or volunteering.

health and emotional well-being are not biologically affected by pregnancy, childbirth, and nursing. This simple fact may help dads keep an even keel as they weather the demands of at-home parenthood.

Yet at-home dads are subject to the same feelings of social isolation as their female counterparts. And while their number is increasing, they're still a novelty in some communities. Some men experience loneliness or prejudice because of their nontraditional role.

Chris, an at-home dad, recently moved with his physician wife, Julie, and their two boys from a small town in New Mexico to a sizeable city in Colorado. One reason they moved was that they believed Chris would find support and social contact from other at-home parents—both moms *and* dads— more easily in an urban area. Sure enough, soon after they settled in, Chris spent hours talking with an at-home dad he met at a McDonald's indoor playground. And Julie met a neighbor family with an at-home dad who said he'd been "disinvited" from two play groups by husbands of at-home moms who apparently feared seduction by the sandbox or canoodling at the kiddie pool.

Brian, an at-home father of two, has found support in parenting education classes and play groups populated largely by women. He says, "It's been a little difficult to find support from the male point of view. I did research and read articles about at-home fathers. I even called some names from a web site, but a lot of them now have older kids.

I've found that males aren't as outgoing with forming groups." Maybe Brian could plan to attend the At-Home Dads Convention held at Oakton Community College in suburban Chicago, which draws about one hundred dads annually for support, learning, and fun.

All at-home parents—moms and dads—need to be aware that they may sometimes feel overwhelmed, undervalued, or alienated from their nonparental selves. You're not a bad parent if you have these feelings! Just think of them as a wake-up call. They're telling you that your situation needs better balance, that your role as a person and partner—not just sandwich maker, diaper changer, and/or milk machine—needs some attention. Seeking balance often means setting aside time just for you— time to pursue something that reminds you who you are besides a parent. Psychologist Robert Frank says matter-of-factly, "No mom or dad should be home alone all day with a child. You've got to do other stuff."

In this chapter we'll explore how at-home parents can identify what gives them energy and joy and schedule those activities into their lives. Parents who get their needs met are parents who can meet the needs of their children. In short, being a good parent means not only caring for others but also caring for you.

Self-Care Strategies for At-Home Parents

You're feeling out of shape. You miss the grown-up world. And let's face it: Your "boss" knows no boundaries! You're always on call and you're not getting paid. You need a coffee break, but you ran out of coffee yesterday, and the car's in the shop. You broke the zipper on your favorite jeans and you can't buy new ones because they're not in this month's budget.

On a day like this, locking yourself in a closet may sound inviting— but in the end, it won't do much for your mental or physical health. Instead, why not try some of the strategies on the following pages to keep your mind and body intact?

Making Connections

The following is a journal entry I wrote during a Labor Day weekend with my husband's family at a lakeside cabin in northern Minnesota. It was the first sunny day after several days of bad weather. Everyone else headed outdoors when the sun appeared. I was inside with my six-week-old daughter, who was napping, and my two-year-old son. I felt trapped.

> ## 4 September 1992
>
> Today I am feeling so left out, so neglected, so tied down that even as I write these words, the tears sting and well up. I liked it better when it was cloudy and rainy and cold, and everyone wanted to stay inside. I feel so guilty asking anyone to watch Benny or listen for Kari, like I'm shirking my duties...I want [my husband] to choose to spend some time with me...I want to hear that I'm wonderful...I want [affirmation]! I try to ask, I try to let him know, but he's got his own needs. *He* doesn't have any problem leaving Kari with someone else.

I'd failed to ask for the help I needed, yet I was feeling very sorry for myself. I also resented my husband's apparent freedom from the kind of emotional baggage I was lugging around. Don't get trapped, as I did, in a quagmire of isolation, self-pity, and resentment. When you start to feel this way, fight the urge to turn inward and reach out to others instead.

The Obvious Choice: Your Coparent

Since that Labor Day a decade ago, I've learned not to overlook the obvious first choice for help—my husband—when I'm feeling stressed out or overwhelmed. He's wonderful about stepping in when I need support, but it's often up to me to ask, since he can't read my mind.

Some couples build "relief parenting" into their schedules. Deb, a stay-at-home mom of two children ages ten and thirteen, says, "One thing that continues to be important to me is that my husband is able to come home at four-thirty and take over." She uses the time to go cross-country skiing with her friends or work on projects that are important to her.

Some Friends Are Silver; Others Are Gold

Cary and her husband, Frank, were the first couple in their circle to have children. Cary found little support among her friends and coworkers for her decision to stay home with her son. She recalls, "Our peers were all saying, 'Can't you think of anything better to do?'" And the women lawyers she worked with as a legal aid assistant "all worked soon after their babies were born." One asked her point-blank, "Aren't you going to be really bored?" So Cary sought support for her decision elsewhere.

She joined a parent education class and found a church where "people get to know your baby and family and watch them grow."

Some parents find that friends don't understand the financial and lifestyle implications of stay-at-home parenting. Lynn and Chuck, parents of two children ages nine and four, sold their suburban Denver home to pay off all of their student loan and credit card debt. For six months they lived in a bus that'd been converted to a small RV so they could save money for a fresh start. "We lost friends over it," says Lynn. "Obviously they weren't great friends. People just couldn't go there with us." But Lynn and Chuck have no regrets; they're thrilled to be debt-free and living in a new home in a small town.

Like Lynn, you might lose friends who can't—or won't—"go there" with you into new parenting territory. Or like Cary, you may find that your work friendships lose their intensity once work is no longer a common bond. Other friendships, too, may fizzle as you turn down invitations once too often or don't reciprocate because you're too tired or simply hoard your downtime by staying close to home. It's natural to circle the wagons when you become a parent. You may go through weeks or even months when you don't want to invest much energy in social activities. It may be all you can do to grab some quiet time for yourself or rent a movie—and stay up late enough to watch it—with your partner.

My circle of friends changed when I became a mother. I gravitated toward people

You Gotta Have Friends

Bee, a work-at-home mom of two, offers this advice: "The most important lesson I learned over the years was to have a support network. It doesn't matter if you're a full-time mother or a part-time professional or if you split shifts with a partner, if you are single or in the middle of a divorce or blissfully partnered. You need some people to talk to and hang out with.... It can be difficult to find the right kinds of friends and may take more effort than a parent of young kids has the energy for, but it's imperative to maintaining sanity and grace in the chaos of parenting."

whose lives resembled mine—who needed to be home for naps or were too exhausted to see a movie after dinner but were always up for morning coffee. And of course that distanced me from some friends with different lifestyles. But not all my preparenthood friendships disappeared. I'm very lucky to have a couple of dear old pals who welcomed my kids with open arms and accommodated my lifestyle. They'd drop over for dinner with something to share and stay to do the dishes; they'd offer to baby-sit; they were content to hang out in my living room instead of going out to a bar or restaurant. Just as the old Girl Scouts camp song says, those old friends are gold to me.

Parenting Teachers and Helpers

Historically, women in family groups and villages raised their children together, sharing moral and practical support. They covered each other both literally and figuratively—from spinning, weaving, sewing, and quilting to making meals and caring for each other's children; from helping with births to mourning deaths; from guiding one another along the Underground Railroad to organizing car pools. Such networks don't exist as organically now as they did in the past. Many people don't know their neighbors well, and extended families often don't live in the same town—much less the same household. Parents who don't have built-in support systems must create their own.

Asking for help may be difficult for introverts and those who see self-sufficiency as a virtue or needing help as a sign of weakness. But most at-home parents say that connecting with others is the key to learning the tricks of the trade. One at-home mom, Geri, insists, "It's a fallacy that parenting is 'natural.'"

No one's born knowing how to be a good parent; parenting is an acquired skill. That's why we must learn from and model ourselves after others—both those who have been through the challenges we're facing and those who are going through them at the same time we are. Your choice to involve or exclude other adults in your life will make or break you as a home-based parent. You need a network of people who understand what you're doing and can offer advice and hands-on help from time to time. Such support can not only help you be a better parent, it can also give you a break when you're desperate, teach your children things you can't share, and help your children learn to trust others besides you.

Try Family First

In about ten percent of mammals, says anthropologist Sarah Blaffer Hrdy, "infant survival depends on the mother being assisted by others—the father and/or various other individuals other than the parents—*alloparents*" or, more precisely, "allomothers—meaning all the caretakers other than the mother."[1]

In other words, family members are the first-choice resource for lots of new parents. This makes sense because "humans have an internal emotional calculus predisposing them to protect, care for, and allocate resources to individuals they classify as kin, their genetic relatives, or those they think of as kin."[2]

Reliable alloparents are a real treasure. My mother is no longer alive, so I can't call her for advice. My dad and brothers live far from me. The aunt with whom I have the closest relationship has no children. But my mother-in-law, who raised six kids and lives twenty minutes from my home, has abundantly provided wisdom and substitute care. My husband's parents and siblings have always been happy to baby-sit and host my kids for sleepovers and outings. I'm extremely lucky to have family around, and I know it. If you don't have this kind of support structure nearby, don't worry. There are lots of great alternatives.

Forge a New "Family"

If you don't have relatives within reach, or if your family just can't provide the support you need, create a substitute family. Build your new family out of friends who are doing what you're doing.

The year I was expecting my first child, I met a woman who had a two-year-old and was expecting her second child. She was a calm and peaceful mother who spoke with joy and conviction about birthing, nursing, and how important these small people are. I asked her lots of questions and listened to and learned from her stories. Our babies were born a month apart, and our families remain friends to this day.

Other parents have similar stories of bonding with others. Bob became best friends with the mom of his son's best friend. Kim got to know a woman who'd gone to business school with her husband but was now staying home. Martha attended La Leche League meetings in her neighborhood and later ran into the same women at preschool and community events. Many of these women are still her friends today, she says.

Singled Out

Maria, a single mom of a five-year-old boy, is her son's primary caregiver during the week. She works weekends while her son is with his father. Finding support as a single mother has been challenging. "My family is very angry with me that I'm divorced," she says and goes on to explain that her family isn't really there for her. "That was a horrible surprise to me."

Although she's resourceful and relies on a strong spirituality to keep herself going when parenting gets tough, that doesn't mean she wants to do it all on her own. Maria reminds coupled parents to reach out to their single counterparts. "It's my personal crusade that single parents need to be counted in things!" Maria says. "We're not all struggling. We're just part of the world and want to be included in things and would like to include you in our things. We're here and we're okay. We're not immediately going to ask you for baby-sitting or money!"

The People in Your Neighborhood

A neighborhood can be a strong source of support for your parenting. Many urban parents I've talked with say cities are especially conducive to at-home parenting because of the high concentration of kid-friendly destinations and resources for meeting people. One mom who lives in a big city says, "I think my sister-in-law [an at-home mom in a small Midwestern town] has it harder."

Urban living has indeed made it easy for me to find support. For example, several women in my neighborhood—some new moms, some veterans—attended the same morning aerobics class at the YMCA a few blocks from our houses. While our children spent an hour in the nursery, one woman taught the class and we all danced and sweated together and traded notes about our experiences as moms.

But urban living isn't always ideal. Another mother says her city neighborhood fell short of her hopes. She'd looked forward to bonding with other families nearby, but those families had different values about parenting or unhealthy dynamics. She and her family welcomed the neighborhood kids into their home and back yard anyway, but she says she grew tired of feeling like the "neighborhood social worker."

If you're not already an at-home parent, you may not be able to predict how well your neighborhood will meet your needs when you make the switch. And even if it's a great fit right now, things can change as families come and go. But it's still worthwhile to investigate whatever resources your neighborhood may have.

If you're currently house-hunting, size up a neighborhood before you make an offer on a house in it. Check it out during the day: Are there parents and kids hanging out? Are there parks with playgrounds nearby? Is there a small business area with a coffee shop, bookstore, or other gathering place? And what about schools, churches, and other community organizations?

In many areas from urban to rural, churches and community centers offer parents' mornings out. Or you might be able to sign up for a parenting education class, where you can learn about your child's development as well as socialize, compare notes, and share ideas with other parents.

Once you've made some connections in your neighborhood, the next step is to nurture them. How do you do that? Make coffee dates or go to the playground together. Trade baby-sitting once a week if your kids are compatible, or start a baby-sitting cooperative.

Parenting Communities

If you don't live in a great neighborhood with natural support systems, if you have a nontraditional family, or if you simply need more structure than an informal block of families, find a local or national parenting organization that meets your needs. There are support networks for parents of all kinds: moms, dads, parents of multiples, single parents, gay and lesbian parents, parents of color, parents of adopted children, parents of

Kid Swaps and Co-Ops

I prefer informal kid swaps with one or two other families at a time. Kid duty can alternate weekly—or even less formally, everybody can just mentally keep track of whose turn it is to have the kids at their home.

Some parents prefer a more structured arrangement that allocates each family a certain number of coupons (valued in hours) used to pay for baby-sitting. When another family watches your child, you pay them with your coupons. When you baby-sit for another family, they pay you. If many families are involved, one may earn coupons by serving as a secretary for the co-op instead of or in addition to baby-sitting.

Baby-sitting co-ops can work with either a handful of families or dozens of families. To keep them running smoothly, it's important to establish policies about things like snacks, meals, diapers, locations, and joining or leaving the co-op.

Source: Peggy Patten, "Babysitting Coops: A Support for Parents in More Ways Than One." *NPIN Parent News,* 7:1 (Jan–Feb. 2001).

children with disabilities, and more. Several such resources are listed on pages 181–82.

Jennifer, a mother of two with a baby on the way, belongs to a local chapter of the International MOMS Club, an organization of local support groups for at-home moms with over fifteen hundred chapters and seventy-five thousand members in seven countries. Such groups are "good for the mother and the child," she says. "They help you get out and make connections and have some sense of community [with other] stay-at-home moms." She's also found opportunities to swap child care with parents she's met through her group.

Electronic communication is another great way to make contact with the wider world. E-mail can be a lifeline to friends and relatives both far and near—and it's incredibly convenient. You can compose e-mails at nap time, after everyone else has gone to bed, when you can't sleep after an early morning feeding, or whenever you can seize a moment. E-mail has helped me reconnect with long-distance college friends I don't see often but love to hear from. Jeanne, another at-home mom, sends a daily communiqué about her two children's activities to both sets of grandparents, who live far away. She also uses the computer to stay informed about current events and issues that matter to her. "My place where I escape," Jeanne says, "is the computer. It's where I relax and my connection to the world."

If you're interested in joining a cyber-community focused on parenting, you'll find many at-home parenting web sites with discussion boards and membership options. Or for a lower-tech morale boost, simply subscribe to a good parenting magazine that offers information on child development, creative solutions to parenting problems, and commentary on issues you care about.

Pages 181–82 lists online, print, and broadcast resources for connecting with other at-home parents. The camaraderie and sense of community you gain from such connections will sustain you on down days—but *you* have to initiate them.

Role Models

My friend Mary says her mother didn't provide the sort of parenting she wanted to emulate, but her mother-in-law has proved to be a wonderful substitute role model. Nanci valued the friendship of a woman with whom she'd gone on canoe trips for years. This woman's three children were about three years older than each of Nanci's. "She was like me. I'd see her every month or so," Nanci says. "She wanted to hear the whole birth story and really listened. I could call her with questions anytime."

In my early years of parenting I learned a lot from friends with older children. There were a few families I observed closely because I admired the parents' way of handling conflict or tough ethical issues, or I admired the children themselves and hoped my kids would turn out like them. Sometimes I asked questions, but often I just listened to parent-child interactions or stories of how the parents handled certain situations. I still observe other families—only these days I pay more attention to conversations about teenagers and high schools than teething and highchairs.

Whether you establish a deliberate relationship with a mentor parent, form a support group, or simply observe parents you think are doing a good job, do seek out parenting role models. Their experiences can serve as guideposts for the behavior and situations you should expect as your kids develop, and their examples can give you ideas about how to handle what's ahead.

Getting Affirmation

All people need to know that what they spend their days doing is valid and valued. At-home parents don't get affirmation from paychecks, performance reviews, or colleagues. And because their work doesn't produce immediate, visible, quantifiable results, they don't always see that what they do makes a difference.

Some at-home parents think no news is good news; in other words, if nobody's complaining, they figure they must be doing a pretty good job. That's probably a safe assumption, but why settle for silence? It can do wonders for one's energy and attitude to hear somebody say, "Honey, I really like the dinner you made tonight," or, "I just want you to know I think you're doing a great job with the kids."

Stay-at-home mom Maggie says one of the things that kept her going was her husband's constant support and affirmation of her role in their family. "Gerry would always talk about how what I was giving the kids was so important," Maggie says. "He said that almost daily. That was really important to me."

Jean Illsley Clarke asserts in her book *Self-Esteem: A Family Affair* that people need affirmation not only for what they do, but also simply for being who they are. In other words, children and adults alike need tangible signs of unconditional love. So just as you'd praise your child or give a high-five for accomplishments like hitting a game-winning home run, improving a math grade, or cleaning his or her room, you'd also offer hands-on evidence that you love your kid "just because": You might greet your kid with a bear hug after school just because you're happy to see him or her, sing a favorite lullaby at bedtime, or say "I love you" every day.

When it comes to themselves, however, parents may suppress their desire for affection or attention or their belief that they deserve it, or they may convince themselves it's selfish to think of their own needs. But paying attention to their emotional health makes them better parents, after all—so it pays off for everyone.

Examine your emotional needs. It's okay to put your need for affection or attention on hold for a short time—say, when your partner is on a quick business trip or your child is sick. But if you make a habit of putting your needs on the back burner, you may have to actively seek ways to get them met. That usually means telling someone what they are and how to meet them. It may seem contrived to ask for a hug, but that may be what you have to do to get it!

Keeping Your Body Healthy

Ask any at-home parent how he or she feels at the end of the day, and you're likely to hear something like this: "I don't know what I did all day, but I'm exhausted!"

At-home parenting, whether you're caring for one baby or several children, is demanding, physical, round-the-clock work. You're bending over, lifting children, perhaps nursing, chasing kids around the yard or playground, running up and down stairs with laundry or groceries, and so on. Though no single task is terribly draining, together they add up to a lot of activity!

To do this demanding job well—and feel well, too—you've got to take care of your body. Make sure your basic needs in the areas of sleep, self-care, exercise, and nutrition get met every day.

Now I Lay Me Down to Sleep

Getting enough sleep is really important. Sure, you can get by for a day or two with less sleep than your body demands, but ignoring your rest requirements for too long can lead to sleep deprivation, which in turn can dramatically affect your physical and mental well-being.

When you have kids, getting an uninterrupted eight hours of sleep can be hard, if not impossible. So get creative and snooze when you can. Pretend you live in a Mediterranean country where people take afternoon siestas, and catch some z's while your child naps. Take turns with your partner waking each night with your child, or alternate nights. Or take turns sleeping in on weekend mornings.

Frumpy, Dumpy, Schlocky, Icky: Self-Care

Many parents report that their self-image takes a hit when they no longer have to go out into the world and mix it up with other adults. There's no getting around it: You'll probably have days when it's hard to look at yourself in the mirror. You're wearing your "fat jeans" and a T-shirt you chose because it was on top of the laundry hamper, not in it. You haven't showered by noon and probably won't until three o'clock, when your kid takes a nap. You haven't exercised for weeks, and all you eat is peanut butter and jelly. You have coffee breath and you're out of clean underwear. You don't even recognize the person with the gray hair and crow's-feet staring back at you from the mirror.

"I find myself using the word *schlocky* to describe myself," says an at-home mom of three. "When you work [outside the home], you have this different self-care routine, makeup, nice clothes…I'm happy to have taken a shower now! I would never have gone out in public looking how I do now."

"I felt like I was in frump mode all the time," echoes another mom, who spent time at home but has now returned to employment. "When you're home, it's hard to get time for yourself. Now that I'm at work, I can sneak off at lunch for a haircut."

You might start thinking that because your appearance is less important to your job performance as an at-home parent than it is for someone who works outside the home, you can afford to let it go. You don't have to show up at the office with your game face on, so you're more likely to pull on a baseball cap instead of washing your hair. Even though you don't have to commute, time is of the essence because you've got to shower before your partner leaves, so you save a few minutes by not shaving. You haven't been able to get to the gym, so you wear sweatshirts to hide the couple of extra pounds you're carrying. (It's a good thing you don't have to wear tailored clothes to do your job, right?)

Though it may be tempting or may even seem necessary to let your appearance go, don't! You deserve to feel good about yourself, so make a point of scheduling self-care into your calendar. Don't feel guilty about hiring a baby sitter, trading child care with a friend, or asking your partner to take charge for a couple of hours so you can have time to do something that recharges your self-image. Get a haircut. Take a long, leisurely bath or shower. Buy some nice lotion or something new to wear.

And when you're having a frumpy, dumpy, schlocky, icky day, be realistic. Remind yourself that not every day before you became a parent was hunky-dory, either.

Exercise Your Right to Exercise

Exercise is the first activity to drop off many new parents' to-do lists, even though it's one of the best things they can do for themselves and their families. It can be hard to carve out time for exercise from a busy family schedule, but the effort pays off in energy and self-esteem for the parent and a good example for the child.

One stumbling block that trips up many parents who'd like to exercise is guilt. They feel funny finding child care just so they can do something for themselves. If this sounds like you, try to dispel any notions of guilt. When you feel good, you're more likely to be a happy, effective parent.

"I'm going to stop using being a mother as an excuse not to take care of myself," declares Martha, who recently weaned her third child and feels ready to get in shape. She's mulling over her strategy. Her NordicTrack has to stay in the basement because it's very noisy and wakes the baby. And she stays up late to get time for herself, so she can't see herself getting up early to exercise. She says she'll figure it out, but she must work through a few real and perceived obstacles first.

I can relate to Martha's situation. After each pregnancy I tried to get back in shape, and it wasn't always easy. It was hard to find time and child care so I could go to the gym or get out for a run or a long walk. Eventually I discovered my neighborhood YMCA. Like many health clubs, it has a nursery for kids whose parents are using the facility. I left my kids there three times a week while I took aerobics classes. It cost me a couple of bucks per class, but it was worth every penny.

It took me longest to resume exercising after my third child was born. Three years later I was still carrying extra weight and I kept making excuses: I needed new running shoes, a running bra, the right kind of clothing to wear. I remember despairing that I would ever run again. In fact, my youngest is now seven, and I just began running three times a week about two and a half years ago. Now that my oldest child is responsible enough to be in charge for a half-hour, my husband and I can run together early in the morning. This routine has become an important fixture in our life, letting us combine exercise with some couple time.

Many families find a sport or other physical activity they can do together. If you bike or run, invest in a bike trailer or baby jogger so you can keep up the habit. My son's friend and his dad take karate together. A mom I know and her three kids all do judo. We like to take bike rides around the extensive trails in our city. Downhill skiing is a great family sport if you can afford it. To keep the cost down, follow the lead of another family I know: They love to ski, but don't want to spend a fortune on lift tickets and equipment. So they buy skis and boots for their growing kids at garage sales, get the cheapest family-rate season pass they can at a

Benefits of Exercise

Now that you're a parent, you definitely want to be around for a while! Exercise that raises your heart rate, such as walking, running, swimming, dancing, biking, and cross-country skiing, decreases total blood cholesterol, blood sugar, and blood pressure. As a result, it also lowers your risk for heart disease, colon cancer, type 2 diabetes, osteoporosis, obesity, and stroke.

Your mood, too, is likely to improve with regular exercise, which affects brain chemistry. Exercise can help you sleep better and increase your stamina. In a survey of regular exercisers, 54 percent said exercise helped their stress levels, and 60 percent said exercise boosted their self-esteem. Exercise can even help treat mild depression.

Here's some great news for busy parents: You don't need to set aside two solid hours to work out! Several short (ten-to-fifteen-minute) bouts of aerobic exercise per day can boost your immune system even more than one longer session. And several short sessions of aerobic, weight-bearing, and flexibility exercises a day, repeated several days a week, provide the same fitness benefits as one longer session each day.

Sources: Phyllis G. Cooper, "Exercise to Stay Healthy," *Clinical Reference Systems* (2001): p. 754.

Carol Krucoff, "Ten Minutes to Fitness," *Saturday Evening Post,* 273:2 (March 2001): p. 28.

Runner's World, 37:4 (April 2002): p. 36.

Prevention, 54:1 (January 2002): p. 64.

●●●●●●●●●●●●●●●●●●●●●

Humor Rx

"We don't laugh because we're happy, we are happy because we laugh."

—*William James*

"Human beings are the only creatures on earth that allow their children to come back home."

—*Bill Cosby*

"Seize the moment. Remember all those women on the *Titanic* who waved off the dessert cart."

—*Erma Bombeck*

local hill, and for a couple hundred bucks, all five of them ski once a week all winter long.

Nutrition Notes

A proper diet is crucial to maintaining good physical and mental health. (See pages 72–81 for a primer on good nutrition for the whole family.) Eating right is especially important for nursing moms. If you're breastfeeding, don't forget that you need more calories than ever. (Women need five hundred more calories per day during lactation than they needed before pregnancy, compared with three hundred extra calories for pregnant women.[3])

Stick to what you know is good for you. I confess to eating more macaroni and cheese and Pop-Tarts than is probably good for me, which I justify by saying I'm in a hurry. Despite my occasional poor choices, I know it pays to get in my five fruits and vegetables a day, my calcium, more water, and less coffee. I always feel better when I do!

Sense of Purpose and Sense of Humor

Consider these your sixth and seventh senses as a parent. They'll help you relinquish perfectionism and look at your work from a healthy perspective.

Keeping the big picture—all the good reasons you've decided to stay home with your child—in mind makes it a lot easier not to sweat the small stuff. It helps you remember that you've chosen to live your life at a particular pace and with particular priorities because of your values.

Stay-at-home mom Linda lives with her teacher husband and their two-year-old son in an affluent East Coast suburb. Cultivating relationships with like-minded friends helps them maintain their commitment to their way of life even though there is subtle pressure to keep up with the Joneses. "We tend to hang around people who have similar priorities as we do, who aren't as interested in gathering money as in being around their kids—not the movers and shakers," says Linda. "I don't feel deprived even though we're in an area where some people have quite a bit of money."

A well-developed sense of humor has saved many a parent's sanity. Learn to laugh at yourself during those crazy moments when the phone's ringing, the baby's crying, your toast is burning, and you've just realized the cat got into your coffee beans. Sometimes you have to let go of the notion that you're in control.

Couple Care

Friends and family can give you key support if you're an at-home parent, but of course your right-hand person in a two-parent family is your partner. Full-time at-home parents need their partners' involvement with child rearing and household work as much as—or perhaps more than—parents in two-earner families. When both parents work outside the home, they're more or less in the same boat. But when one's the breadwinner and the other's the bread baker, they're living very different lives. They may have to work harder to understand and help each other.

Moral Support

Maggie says her four years at home had both blissful and bleak moments. When she felt disconnected from the wider world or yearned to break out of her role, her husband, Gerry, often reminded her that the years of parenting young children wouldn't last forever. "He gave me perspective," Maggie says. Gerry helped her remember that in five years, that wasn't what she'd be doing.

Maggie believes it's very important for the parent who's not at home to spend some time in a role reversal. She says a weekend day or one evening a week alone with the kids can help the at-home parent's partner "really, truly be supportive."

Letting Go

Even if you dream every day of walking away from it all when your partner comes home from work, even if you fantasize about escaping to a solitary beach or mountaintop after a hard day of being your child's primary caregiver, relinquishing "your" job to your partner can be stressful! You may worry about your partner's ability to meet your child's needs and manage the household as well as you. You may think everything will fall apart if the routine you've established isn't followed. Don't be afraid to let go and let your coparent do things his or her way. Remember: He or she loves your child just as much as you do and deserves to learn, as you have, how to be the best possible parent.

The Value of Having a Parent at Home

Experienced at-home parents say that both partners must agree on the value of having a parent at home, or the arrangement probably won't work. Unresolved tensions and questions must be addressed.

Many parents supporting at-home partners experience changes in their identity. Some assume the mantle of provider; others find they want to take on more nurturing than they'd imagined; still others feel excluded from the intimate relationship between at-home parent and child.

Some wage-earning parents give lip service to the value of at-home parenting because they think it will make their partners happy or because *they* grew up with parents at home. But if the wage earner harbors resentment about a reduced income, having a partner who's not a professional, coming home every night to a spouse in sweats, or switching traditional roles, serious conflict can ensue. If these issues sound familiar to you, be sure to discuss them thoroughly—and soon—with a counselor's help if necessary.

Kim believes her stint as an at-home mother was good for her children, but she admits, "It didn't do great things for my marriage." Kim's focus was on the kids, and she says her husband "didn't value that the same way I did." He sent mixed messages about whether he really wanted her to stay home, which contributed to her uncertainty about her role. "Whenever we'd have an argument, he'd tell me to get a job," she says.

In Linda's experience, "The pressure [on at-home parents] isn't societal, but in the relationship. There's a need to redefine your goals and renegotiate the terms of your family life. People change. You ought to be open to that. I wish Tom and I talked more about that. It would make it easier."

"The key," advises Kim, "is that you both have similar expectations." Talk about those expectations and ask each other questions if you feel any doubt or confusion. Open communication will help you build your at-home arrangement on solid ground instead of the shifting sands of assumption. Here's a short list of questions to get you started:

- Does the wage earner expect dinner on the table and a spotless house?
- Does the at-home parent expect relief from kid duty the instant the wage earner walks in the door after work?
- Are weekends for downtime or doing errands and household projects?
- How much time alone does each parent need?
- How much time with friends does each parent need?
- And most importantly: What's the value of having an at-home parent?

Time Together
Let's assume you and your partner agree on the value of having a parent at home, you know how to support each other and when to let go, and you've negotiated mutually acceptable terms of family life. Whether you have one primary caregiver or you're sharing the job, you're bound to find yourselves playing tag-team at some point. If you're talking to each other only long enough to hand off your child or rattle off a list of errands and falling into bed exhausted at night, you might forget how you got to be parents in the first place! Don't let that happen; instead, make a serious investment in couple time.

Leave Guilt Outside with the Garbage
Guilt about planning couple time has no place in your home. It belongs outside with the other emotional garbage you clear out when you become a parent.

William Doherty, director of the marriage and family therapy program at the University of Minnesota and author of *Take Back Your Kids* and *Take Back Your Marriage*, says demonstrating a solid, loving marriage is the best thing parents can do to foster a healthy family life. Adults need time to talk, to do things they enjoy together, to be alone with each other. They don't need to focus every moment on their children's needs or permit

One Good Turn Deserves Another

Having a parent at home may actually increase parental comfort about insisting that children respect couple time. Dave, who has worked part-time at home since his teenage daughters were in first and third grades, says, "My relationship with Becky is very important. We've always made sure we have time for the two of us, even at the expense of the girls. It's not any huge thing, like taking a week's vacation, but little times during the day when we want time together" to find out how each other's day went, discuss current events, or simply enjoy a quiet moment in each other's presence. Dave spends time with his daughters before school, picks them up after school, and shuttles them to swimming, soccer, and Girl Scouts. He muses that if he's available to them exclusively a couple of hours each morning and afternoon, "there has to be some kind of reciprocity."

kids to incessantly interrupt adult conversation. In fact, Doherty says, doing so is detrimental to kids because it creates a sense of entitlement; children begin to think their needs *always* come first. Many couples confirm that failure to make time for communicating and relaxing together can spell trouble for an at-home parenting arrangement.

Doherty claims that rituals are as important for couples as they are for families. (See pages 102–03 for more on family rituals.) In *Take Back Your Kids,* he describes one couple ritual he and his wife practiced: After supper, their children ate dessert while mom and dad washed the dishes and started a pot of coffee. Then they sent the kids to play while they spent fifteen minutes over coffee talking one-on-one. If the children interrupted, "we gently told them to wait because we were having our coffee talk." When told of this nightly ritual, other parents had a hard time believing that kids could cooperate like that for fifteen minutes. Doherty says it's a matter of expectations. "If you start when the children are young, it seems natural to them.... They can be taught to respect and support the boundaries of [their parents' marriage]."[4]

Date Night
It can be hard to plan—not to mention pay for—regular dates with your partner. For starters, the wage-earning and at-home parents may want to spend their precious kid-free time in different ways. The at-home parent might be itching to get out of the house for a movie or dinner, while the parent

who's just spent the day in meetings and rush-hour traffic might want to crash on the couch with a rented video.

Then there's the cost: You can fork over an incredible sum just to go out for an evening. In 2003, a baby sitter for four hours can cost anywhere from twenty to forty bucks, dinner for two at a moderate restaurant is about fifty dollars, and two movie tickets at a first-run theater cost fifteen to twenty dollars. That's eighty-five to one hundred dollars for one night out!

BABY BLUES   BY RICK KIRKMAN & JERRY SCOTT

© Baby Blues Partnership. Reprinted with special permission of King Features Syndicate.

Sometimes it doesn't seem worth the expense. But remember that your partnership is more than a business arrangement. You and your sweetie need to connect with each other as two adults who have something in common besides your child. Even a really tight budget is no excuse to skip spending time together. Dates don't have to be expensive, just exclusive

Eight Great You-Time Ideas

Here are some popular ways to remind yourself that the earth does not revolve around Disney, peanut butter, and dinosaurs, and that you have your very own interests and needs.

1. *Volunteer.* All it takes is a phone call. Churches, social service providers, arts organizations, and schools all need volunteers and would surely love to put your skills to good use. As you make inquiries, ask if child care is available.

2. *Take a class.* Community education classes are usually quite cheap and cover everything from flower arranging to car repair to Freudian psychology.

3. *Join a book club.* Or start one! It needn't be a huge time commitment, and it'll give you intellectual stimulation and adult conversation in one fell swoop.

4. *Deal with your own issues.* See a therapist or a spiritual director for guidance along the path of parenthood. One mom with seventeen years of sobriety under her belt says her Alcoholics Anonymous meeting is the one thing she never misses. Another goes to Al-Anon.

(adults only). Go to a matinee or a discount theater and out for coffee. Have a picnic instead of going to a restaurant. Take a walk together or go ice skating. Or check out pages 51–52 for lots more cheap date ideas.

When our children were younger and our budget tighter, my husband and I had dinner dates at home instead of going out. We fed the kids early, then put them to bed and made another meal for ourselves—often seafood or something we liked, but the kids didn't. We set the table with candles, put on a favorite CD, and cracked open a bottle of wine. We really enjoyed these evenings and felt good about treating ourselves without blowing our budget.

Despite the difficulty you may have planning dates, they're worth the effort. They strengthen your couple relationship, which is the foundation of your family. Ideally, you might spend time together once a week with no kids around—and an agreement not to talk about them! But realistically, every other week or even once a month may be all you can manage. "The marriage is a huge piece to tend," says Cary. She and her husband Frank eventually learned to spend time alone together at least once a week. "We'd go to dinner and a movie. There were periods when that was the most we could do, so we didn't see other people socially."

Whatever you plan, be sure to write it on your calendars and make it a priority. Remember that the time you spend with each other will help you keep alive the shared values, dreams, and attractions that brought you together in the first place.

Time Just for You

For many at-home parents, getting time for themselves is even lower on the priority list than planning couple time. It's easy to forget or avoid squeezing time for yourself into a schedule already crammed with the demands of family life and household management. But here's my advice: Do it anyway.

Doing things you enjoy and are good at reinforces your self-image. It helps you remember that you're a productive person with unique talents, skills, and interests. Pursuing your interests kid-free also does wonders to combat boredom and infuse your parenting with new energy. If you make time to do something that reminds you of who you are besides a mom or dad, you'll be a better and happier parent for it.

Geri, an at-home mom with two sons ages four and eight, recalls a low point when her first-born was two years old: "I was feeling very isolated and struggling with depression. I felt like every time I spoke to an adult, I would babble," she said. "I credit my husband with identifying my need. He said, 'You need more than four walls.'"

Geri loves gardening, so she approached a local garden center to ask if they ever hired "part-part-time" help. They did, and she began to work ten hours a week seasonally, mainly on weekends when her husband was home. "It was very people-oriented, and I was doing something I loved and wanted to learn more about," said Geri. Most importantly, her job did not require her to choose between family and work. She could reserve

5. *See a play or concert.* Buy a subscription or season pass so you have "automatic" dates with your partner or a friend. Or buy low-cost "rush" seats.

6. *Get a job.* Make it a part-part-time one. One dad lifeguards on the early morning shift. A mom works at a garden center. Another sells kids' clothes.

7. *Indulge yourself.* Allow small luxuries that bring you a little joy, no matter how tight your budget. Fresh flowers. A really nice bar of soap. A good chocolate bar. A new CD. A subscription to *Vanity Fair, Sports Illustrated,* or *The Atlantic Monthly.* Funky socks or sunglasses. Red lipstick. Blue nail polish.

8. *Pursue an interest.* Get your creative juices flowing somehow. Draw, journal, listen to music, make music, garden, cook something special, read a novel. If you don't have time for a novel, read a poem.

the bulk of her time for her family, which remained her primary commitment. As her boys have gotten older, she's added yoga, cross-country skiing, and running to her schedule. She says she finds satisfaction—as well as mental health and physical energy—by keeping physically fit.

Nanci, another stay-at-home mom, recommends that all at-home parents find time every day, even if it's only ten minutes, to be by themselves. Do something—or nothing. Work out. Read a book. Get a manicure. Volunteer. Paint. Write. See a movie. Get together with friends. Go to the library when it's not story time. Walk the dog without a stroller in tow. Write in a journal. Lock yourself in the bathroom if you need to (provided your child is supervised or old enough not to need supervision, of course). One mother told me of an "introverted" friend whose big escape from her three children, who were very close in age, was to take a bowl of cereal into the bathroom and eat it—all alone!

Blending Your "Before" and "After" Identities

Almost every at-home parent struggles to redefine his or her identity and come up with a statement to present to the rest of the world. How you redefine yourself is a highly personal matter on which I can't even begin to advise you. It depends, of course, on where you've been, where you are now, and your goals for the future. Though I can't give you a blueprint for this remodeling job, I can show you a few examples of how other at-home parents have met the challenge.

The Contemplative Approach

Mary Dee says the hardest aspect of quitting her high-level job as an organizational consultant is "isolation and loss of community." She has replaced her professional interactions with a lot of quiet time alone, which she believes is exactly what she needs at this point in her life.

Mary Dee replenishes her energy for her family by reading in her field of psychology, pursuing personal interests like piano and gardening, and writing a book about the experiences of women like her. "It's not possible to engage in a fundamental reevaluation of how you want to be in the world without space," she explains. "I'm going forward to somewhere, but I don't know where. There's still a lot I want to contribute to other people, to professional discourse."

So What if There's a Diaper in My Pocket?

Laurie spends most of her time at home with her three children, but she also does a few hours of telephone consulting each week and volunteers on a local government board to stay connected to the legal community. "I don't want to totally lose my lawyer identity," she says.

As a community volunteer she meets regularly with an executive committee of "high-level" professionals. "Meetings are scheduled during the workday, of course, and often changed at the last minute," she says. "I have to pay ten dollars an hour for child care and make arrangements to pick my kids up, or maybe I've just come from a play date, or the meeting [time or venue] gets changed. I often have to run late or leave early. I feel bad about that. In a way it's a lowered standard of professionalism, like there's always a diaper in my pocket," she jokes. But she also feels, "So what? These people need to be reminded that this is reality for many people."

Parenting as a New Source of Creativity

Nanci was an actor before she left the stage because it conflicted with her parenting goals. In the middle of the night, while patting her baby back to sleep, she came up with the idea of a radio show for moms and by moms. She then figured out a way to blend her mom identity with her performing skills via *MOMbo*, an award-winning radio show dedicated to the everyday work of mothering and to giving an honest voice to the diverse experiences of motherhood. The weekly show aired locally in Minneapolis–Saint Paul for six years and nationally on the Pacifica Radio Network for five years.

Though *MOMbo* no longer airs weekly, Nanci continues to produce special shows, which are distributed nationwide by Public Radio International. She's also a commentator on other public radio programs and a writer for various national parenting journals and http://www.mombo.org.

Seeking Professional Help

Though there are lots of effective ways at-home parents can care for themselves, sometimes they need a little extra help. If they have negative feelings about themselves, their families, or their situations, it doesn't mean they're being unreasonable, that they've made the wrong decision, or that

Love Your Kids. Be Good to Yourself.

Nanci Olesen closes each *MOMbo* program with this motto. Here's a review of the most important ways at-home moms and dads can be good to themselves:

- *Ask for help.* Call a friend. Join a support group. Talk to your partner about sharing your workload.
- *Take care of the basics.* Make sure you get sufficient sleep, self-care, exercise, and good nutrition every day.
- *Laugh.* Laugh at yourself, at life, with your kids, with your friends, with your partner.
- *Cut yourself some slack.* Forgive yourself for not having a perfectly clean house or matching socks.
- *Connect with your partner.* Make sure you get regular time together with no kids around.
- *Connect with yourself.* Make sure you get regular time with no kids *or* partner around.

they aren't good at the job. Such feelings are common—but it's important to remember that sometimes they signal mental health concerns requiring professional intervention.

Postpartum Emotional Problems

All women who've recently given birth experience emotional ups and downs. Causes include hormone fluctuation, fatigue, inexperience, isolation, infant demands, difficult or disappointing birth experiences, unexpected health problems, stressful circumstances (financial, relationship, and so on), and/or personal or family history of mood disorders.[5]

For about 80 percent of new moms, the ups and downs are relatively mild and short-lived, appearing within the first week after giving birth and lasting about a week. Symptoms of such "baby blues" include feeling overwhelmed, out of control, exhausted, anxious, sad, and inadequate, and crying easily. They're usually alleviated by getting more rest, reducing physical pain, and getting more support from family and friends.[6]

About 20 percent of women experience one of four more serious, longer-lasting emotional conditions called postpartum mood disorders (PPMDs), which are described in the sidebar on page 141. PPMDs usually appear within two months after giving birth but may occur anytime during the first year. Women with PPMDs often benefit from professional help. Treatment depends on the symptoms and their severity;

it may include lifestyle changes, therapy, and/or medication.[7]

A tiny percentage of new mothers—about one in one thousand—suffer from postpartum psychosis, a condition that causes them to lose touch with reality. (See the sidebar at right for symptoms.) The highly publicized case of Andrea Yates, a Houston mother who killed her five children in 2001, is an example of this severe condition. Postpartum psychosis usually appears soon after birth and requires immediate treatment by a psychiatrist. Victims of postpartum psychosis are often hospitalized initially and given medication to treat their symptoms. When they return home, they usually continue medication and outpatient psychotherapy.[8]

Beyond the Baby Blues

For some parents, feelings of inadequacy, low self-esteem, anger, or depression surface only after months or even years of the daily demands of small children. Like PPMDs, they can often be relieved by lifestyle adjustments, medication, and/or therapy.

Mary, a mother of three teens, recalls her experiences after eighteen months at home with her three children, who were born within a four-year span. She'd quit her accounting job when her third child was born. The family's trusted daycare provider had recently died of cancer, and looking for a new provider—not to mention affording daycare for three kids—seemed too difficult. Having an at-home mom seemed like the

Get Professional Help for These Symptoms

Postpartum Mood Disorders

- *Postpartum anxiety and panic disorder:* Shortness of breath, choking sensations, faintness, rapid heart rate, chest pain, nausea, diarrhea, fear of being alone, fear of dying, fear of baby dying, fear of leaving home.

- *Postpartum obsessive-compulsive disorder:* Repeated, uncontrollable thoughts, speech, and rituals that interfere with normal daily living.

- *Postpartum depression:* Feelings of hopelessness, exhaustion, inadequacy, and low self-esteem; loss of interest in everything; angry outbursts; thoughts of harming self or baby; sleeplessness; forgetting to eat or overeating; constant crying.

- *Postpartum posttraumatic stress disorder:* Flashbacks, recurrent nightmares, rage, extreme protectiveness, anxiety, panic attacks.

Postpartum Psychosis

- Severe agitation, mood swings, depression, and delusions.

Source: Penny Simkin, Janet Whalley, and Ann Keppler, *Pregnancy, Childbirth, and the Newborn,* Meadowbrook Press (2001): pp. 377–78.

right strategy for Mary's family. But a year and a half at home with her children sent Mary into a clinical depression.

"Being alone with three kids four and under at home was way too hard," she says. She describes her confused identity: "It got totally overwhelmed with taking care of the needs of…little kids. I just lost my ability to fight for myself." She recalls that she was unable to get out of the house regularly and muses, "I should've been able to ask [my husband] for money for child care."

Mary finally saw a doctor and a therapist when she began to feel she might hurt herself or her kids. She took prescribed antidepressants as well as the therapist's advice that she "*needed* to get away from the kids periodically." She found someone to watch the children for a couple of hours a week and started biking, an activity she'd enjoyed before she had kids. She also began to work part-time as a bookkeeper.

"I took a job for five-fifty an hour to save my life!" she says, laughing. The job's flexible hours and location just a few blocks from her house let her spend most of her time with her children—which, despite her troubles, remained her top priority—while she reclaimed her professional identity and personal space.

One Last Thought

It's probably inevitable that sometimes you'll put yourself last. Just don't do it *all* the time. And remember: Your children really will get older and more independent. I considered three the magic age. When each of my children turned three, I somehow felt my burden had lightened. There was no more diaper changing, they slept and ate well, they could occupy themselves independently at least for short periods of time, and it was much easier to leave them in someone else's care. And best of all, I started to feel like myself again—only better and wiser than ever because of my experience.

Chapter 5

Nitty-Gritty

Parenthood is simultaneously sublime and…well…earthy. When you welcome your sweet, cuddly baby into your home, you also invite a future filled with stinky diapers, piles of laundry, sinks full of dishes, sticky handprints, muddy shoes, spills and breaks and other household destruction, collections of rocks or string or baseball cards, photos that must be put into albums, and so on. Managing the space and stuff in your home becomes more important than ever.

There's also managing time and information. You know, like adhering to a baby's eating and sleeping schedules, monitoring everyone's clean underwear supply and library due dates, noticing that you're almost out of mayonnaise and flour, and remembering that one kid's piano lesson was switched to Tuesday while the other kid doesn't have ballet on Friday but has a sleepover instead.

Managing a family's logistics is a big job that often falls on the shoulders of at-home parents. Some people have assistants to help them do this job in their work lives! Though I can't hire you a personal assistant, I can give you some information and advice that will hopefully help you navigate the nitty-gritty of your new life as an at-home parent.

Time Management

Drawing Boundaries
The first several months with a new baby are bound to be chaotic. You're probably sleep-deprived and a bit overwhelmed by your new responsibilities, and your entire life revolves around your baby's often unpredictable needs. Out of this chaos a pattern eventually emerges: Your child begins to sleep and eat at fairly predictable intervals. When this happens, you can reclaim some control over your time. You'll be able to give more attention to the tasks of daily living and organize your day into manageable segments.

Perhaps you're the kind of parent who can talk on the phone and write up a grocery list while feeding a baby. Or maybe you prefer to concentrate on one thing at a time. (I've got news for you: At some point you'll have to learn to multitask!) Whatever your personality, you'll probably find that having a few overall boundaries or rules on how you spend your time helps you stay sane and allows you to focus on the important stuff. Here are some suggestions:

- If the phone rings while you're in the middle of something, whether it's a crisis or a precious moment, let your answering machine or voice mail get it. Remember: The phone and its features are there for *your* convenience, not vice versa.

- You might find computer work less stressful and more productive when your child is not around—maybe during nap time, after bedtime, or when your partner has kid duty. If you work at home, consider keeping regular hours while your child is occupied at school or with a sitter.

- Don't worry too much about doing housework while your child needs your attention. Housework will always be there, but your child won't!

- Make nap time sacred in your home. (For more on this, see pages 98–100.) If you need a nap while your child is sleeping, go for it. Otherwise, use the quiet time for yourself or to do tasks that are difficult with kids underfoot. You might give yourself fifteen or thirty minutes of complete quiet to do anything you want, then move on to your round of duties.

Do your best to enforce the boundaries you've drawn, but remember that you may need to adapt them as your needs or your child's needs change.

Evaluating Commitments
Some parents try to maintain the same pace of involvement in community, church, or social activities after having kids as they did before kids. You *can* do a lot with kids in tow. But most parents eventually reach a point at which enough is enough, and they realize it's imperative to cut back in order to respect their child's—not to mention their own—need for adequate sleep, regular meals, and that unscheduled time when life happens.

I let go of all volunteer commitments when my first child was born. I didn't know how to be a mom and I knew I needed time to learn. As the years have passed, I've had two more children and become a more confident parent, my kids have grown older and more self-sufficient, and I've gradually added activities back into my life. I served as an advisor to a group of young adult volunteers. I became a member of my parish council. I joined a book club.

Though my children can now make their own lunches and dinners, put themselves to bed, and even stay home alone for short periods of time, that doesn't mean I've automatically continued to add outside activities. In fact, I think it's more important than ever to periodically reevaluate my commitments and let go of the ones that no longer fit my schedule or my priorities. I'm constantly trying to balance my time in the private sphere of home, family, and personal interests with my time in the public sphere of work, social, church, and school activities. The mantra *one day at a time* has saved my sanity more than once. Sometimes I've even amended it to *one hour at a time* or *five minutes at a time.*

Living off the Clock

Time: Enemy and Ally

When you stop punching a time clock or filling a day planner, you may revel in your newfound freedom—or you may experience a serious time warp.

Learning to Draw Boundaries

Nanci Olesen, mother of three, produces and hosts a radio show for moms called *MOMbo*. (For more info on *MOMbo*, see page 139.) Her background also includes acting, puppetry, and circus work.

When Olesen and her husband had their first child, they were both working as actors. Their schedules revolved around daytime rehearsals and evening performances. She says that one of the first things she learned from her artist friends about having kids was to incorporate her child into her life instead of compartmentalizing. She calls this "a potluck view of life."

Throughout her son Henry's first year, Olesen brought him to rehearsals, swapped child-care duties with friends (even, with a kindred mom, nursing the other's baby if necessary), and chipped in with another actor to pay a home daycare provider who worked evenings. But eventually she realized that her extremely flexible approach to parenting was starting to compromise her son's need for routine, especially at bedtime.

"It became clear that having two actors wasn't going to work. I was a mom interested in a scheduled life for my child," Olesen says. So she quit the stage to pursue interests more compatible with her new role as a parent. She schedules her work at home and in the radio studio to balance with her children's school schedule. "I turn off the computer at four o'clock, when they come home from school, and until they're in bed, I don't do anything related to *MOMbo*." Except be a mom, that is.

Time is a tyrant when you're playing your nineteenth round of Candy Land, pacing the floor with a baby, or desperately waiting for your partner to return home at the end of the day so you can get a few minutes to yourself. There are times when you're sure a half-hour has passed, but when you work up the nerve to look at the clock, you discover it's only been five minutes, and you wonder if the darn thing needs new batteries. You may pine for that day planner or timecard.

On the other hand, living off the clock can be a boon to your peace of mind. Some at-home parents feel that one of the biggest benefits of the job is the ability to live more in tune with kid time, taking life as it comes and flexibly moving from one activity to the next. "For me the real joy of staying at home is that my life is not operated by the clock," says Deb, mother of two kids ages thirteen and ten. "I've found staying home with my children to be an incredibly spiritual experience. It has forced me to live in the moment." Parents like Deb value spending as much time as possible accomplishing their children's agendas, which are likely to include such important activities as sitting on the front porch drinking lemonade on summer afternoons, taking long walks around the block, or spending hours at the sandbox.

Geri relished days when she and her sons could watch construction vehicles at work or draw a chalk line around the entire block. Marian, who was home with her children until a midafternoon switch with her husband, Doug, says her mornings with the kids had a leisurely pace that tangibly shifted by early afternoon, when she had to begin getting ready for work.

Linda, who has two school-age daughters, left her job as a partner in a law firm and now does freelance work from her home. Her husband, also a lawyer, works long hours and doesn't help much with household management and tasks such as grocery shopping, cooking, dishes, cleaning, bills, laundry, and walking the dog. (He didn't when she worked full-time either.) Linda's increased hours at home and decreased stress level enhance her family's quality of life. "We set the table and eat real food," Linda says, "and when the kids are around after school, I can talk to them and listen to them. I've always liked large margins around things. I need transition time. I feel it's unfair to kids to not let them have that, too."

Brian, at home with his two-year-old and infant daughters, says his presence at home has really reduced tensions there. The stress induced by a schedule of daycare drop-off and pickup (especially when providers charge extra for tardiness), deadlines, traffic jams, and other work-related factors has been very low for his family. He comments, "We still rush sometimes, but not on a daily basis. That type of thing—high stress or low stress—gets absorbed by the kids."

Avoiding the Rush

If there's one thing that can make a parent break down, it's trying to get ready and get out the door to go somewhere on a schedule. Though I'm constantly trying to improve my on-time record, I'm not exactly known for my promptness. I can understand why people run late: They overbook themselves and underestimate travel and transition time. And as a mom of three, I also understand why people with children are even less reliable: Sometimes getting everyone out of the house feels like herding cats!

Ideally, I think parents should avoid imposing their sense of time pressure on children. Children simply do not understand time the way adults do, and it's virtually useless to rush them by nagging or yelling, which only makes everyone feel bad. At-home parents can take advantage of greater flexibility in their schedules and learn to work on kid time. Here's a hint: Add at least fifteen minutes to the time you think you'll need to get anywhere with a kid.

Hints for Handling the Clock Monster

Here are a few tips to help kids handle time-sensitive situations and stay on task without rushing them and adding stress to everyone's day.

- If your child is able to grasp the concept of time, you could give a ten-minute warning, then a five-minute warning along with a short list of what you expect him or her to do before leaving home: for example, brush teeth and hair and put on shoes.
- Set a timer to announce departure time. This relieves you of the role of "enforcer."
- Give your child an alarm clock and teach him or her how it works.
- If all else fails, let your child experience the natural consequences of tardiness, such as missing the school bus. Sometimes simple embarrassment at being late provides enough incentive to avoid the situation again.
- Before your child goes to bed, have him or her get ready for the morning. My older daughter was described by her preschool teacher as "a child who will not be hurried." She's now in fifth grade, and to this day she's often the last one out of bed and dawdles as she gets ready for school. To avoid problems in the morning, we encourage her at night to pack her backpack, set out her clothes, and gather her swimsuit, flute, piano books, or whatever gear she'll need for her after-school activities the next day.

What takes so long? For parents of babies, any outing requires packing enough gear for an Antarctic expedition: diaper bag, car seat, change of clothes, bottle or snack, stroller, appropriate outerwear, and so on. And of course as soon as everything's ready, baby has a diaper blowout, and it's back to square one. For parents of toddlers, preschoolers, and even primary graders, the delay has a different cause: These kids simply don't share their parents' sense of urgency. They get engrossed in what they're doing or get distracted along the way. They know they need to brush their teeth to get ready for school…but on the way to the bathroom, they remember they have to feed the bird…only they need to find a spoon to scoop the bird food…and when they get to the kitchen, they realize they forgot to eat breakfast and go the refrigerator for a bagel….

In or Out

Just as time can be friend or foe to stay-at-home parents, so can the home they spend their time in! If the personalities of parent and child call for it, families may prefer to organize their days around staying in or going out.

Relishing Days at Home

As the head of a county human services planning agency, Jeanne worked fifty-to-sixty-hour weeks before quitting her job to be at home with her infant daughter and preschooler son. She's still deeply involved in the community. She does lots of volunteer computer and telephone work during her children's naps and sometimes attends weekend or evening meetings.

Jeanne's daily routine with her children has quite a different flavor from her organized community work. In the course of an hour she'll pretend with her son that he's a puppy, play with trains or a dollhouse, and set up watercolor paints. She nurses her daughter on demand, with classical music playing on the radio in her living room.

"I relish days at home," says Jeanne. "Our play time is really unstructured. I don't fret over goals for the day or anything."

Outward Bound

Some parents go stir-crazy from the slower pace of life at home with children—especially young children. They may need to schedule daily activities that bring them into contact with other adults: meeting a friend at a coffee shop, exercising at the club while baby is in the facility's child-care room, signing up for a parent-child activity class, taking baby to the grocery store, setting up a play group, and so on. (For more ideas on outings and making connections with other adults, see pages 93–95 and 117–25.)

"I like to do stuff all the time," says Kim, a former at-home mom who has returned to work as an attorney. Kim spent a lot of one-on-one time with her two-year-old son while her four-year-old daughter was in school every morning. They went regularly to the library, arranged play dates, did errands, and got together with other moms and kids in her neighborhood. But she got bored in the afternoons, when both children napped. "I'd be sitting there folding laundry and watching *General Hospital*," she says, "and going nuts!"

What Works for Your Family?

Here are some questions and ideas that'll help you establish a routine that suits your family's unique personalities, values, and needs. (For more advice on establishing family routines, see pages 96–98.)

Factors to Consider

Some factors affecting a family's routine are *temperamental*. For example:

- Are you and your child early or late risers?
- When does your child nap?
- If your child is a baby, when is his or her fussy time?
- Do your family members like to have a lot of or a little transition time between activities?
- How much unstructured time do you and your child like?

Other factors are *external*. For example:

- When does your partner leave for and return from work?
- Do you have any evening commitments?
- What time is your child's favorite TV show on? (Not that I advocate planning one's day around TV, but if you know you'll need some quiet time, a high-quality children's program can help you get it.)
- If you have a child in school, when does he or she get off the school bus (or arrive home or need to be picked up)?

- What activities does your child participate in? Do you need to limit these to preserve some family time?

Still other factors are based on your family's *values:*

- Is it important to attend religious services regularly?
- Is it important to eat dinner together every night?
- Is it important to participate in sports?
- Is it important to volunteer in the community?

Budget Time Just Like Money

Creating a family budget helps you use your finite financial resources in the most effective way possible. Budgeting time is just as important as budgeting money. The time you have each day is finite, too, so spend it wisely!

Get a big calendar and write down all your family's activities—doctor appointments, car-pool commitments, piano lessons, late work nights, meetings, social events, library due dates, and so on. The more complete your calendar is, the better. Meet with your partner weekly or monthly to make sure everything is accurately noted. If you like, write each family member's activities in a different color.

Looking at a calendar will help you get a feel for the rhythm of your daily and weekly routine. Just seeing your schedule on paper may help you feel in control of it—or may help you see where you can fine-tune it for better balance. For example, if your six-o'clock yoga class is really important to you, but you haven't been able to attend since your baby's birth because your partner gets home from work too late, maybe he or she could arrange to leave for work and come home earlier on your class days. Or maybe you could attend an early morning class while your partner is home with the baby.

I use a traditional paper calendar because I need to schedule things months in advance, and I often need to check a previous month to see when I paid a bill, got a haircut, or attended an event. If you prefer, you might use an erasable calendar, which is more environmentally friendly and perhaps less expensive in the long run. Both types of calendars come in large sizes suitable for busy families with lots of activities. Some parents I know use business tools like day planners and personal digital assistants

(PDAs). A PDA tracks appointments electronically, issues audible reminders, and can be synchronized with a desktop or laptop computer's address book and calendar.

Just when you think you've got a schedule down, you can be sure some unpredictable event will interfere: School is canceled due to a blizzard, somebody calls with a last-minute offer of tickets to a children's play, your car breaks down, your dog throws up and needs to see the vet, you get a call from a client and must take it. So go ahead and plan your time, but always expect the unexpected!

Household Management

Whether your style is top-drawer or junk-drawer, you must have *some* system of organizing and maintaining your space and stuff at home, just as you would anywhere else you might work. I admire those who have "a place for everything and everything in its place." I, too, have a place for everything and can tell you where any item in our house may be located. My directives usually sound something like this: "Check on top of that pile of papers next to the laundry basket on the third stair."

Okay, so I'm working on it. Here are a few things I've gleaned over the years about household management.

Record Keeping

Keeping track of important household documents in a systematic way can save you tons of time and stress when you need those documents for whatever reason. If you don't already have a good record-keeping system, now's a great time to establish one. It needn't be big or elaborate; just easy to find and navigate.

First, designate a desk drawer, file box, cabinet, or other spot in your home for documents that are easy and/or inexpensive to replace. Obtain a safe-deposit box at your bank for records that are difficult and/or expensive to replace. Then gather all your family, property, financial, and legal records. Review them one by one and use the following list to help you decide which documents to toss, which to keep, and where to keep them. (Remember: It's up to you to judge the importance of your unique documents.) You should update most household documents periodically and keep them indefinitely.

Household Records Checklist

Keep at Home

- Education histories
- Employment histories
- Contact information for family medical, legal, financial, and/or spiritual advisors
- Insurance policies (Keep until policies expire.)
- Health records
- Copies of licenses to practice (Display originals at practice site.)
- Guarantees and warranties (Keep until no longer valid.)
- Household inventory (Record items, costs, and dates of purchase.)
- Instruction manuals (Keep until you dispose of products.)
- Mortgage records
- Bank account books, statements, and/or canceled checks (Keep for five years.)
- Creditor names, addresses, and account numbers
- Home improvement records (Keep for three years after reporting sale of home on income tax return.)
- Receipts for important purchases, budgeting, or filing income taxes
- Tax returns (Keep at least five years.)
- Copy of will, living will, and/or power of attorney (Keep originals with attorney.)
- Government bond dates, serial numbers, denominations, co-owners, and amounts received when redeemed
- Pension and profit-sharing plan records
- List of safe-deposit box contents

Keep in Safe-Deposit Box

- Birth certificates and/or adoption papers
- Records of religious rites
- Proof of citizenship

- Passports
- Copyrights and/or patents
- Death certificates
- Divorce decrees
- Marriage records
- Military records
- Copies of social security cards
- List of insurance policies (Include policy number, name of insured, beneficiary, company, and agent for each policy.)
- Copy of household inventory
- Real estate abstracts and deeds (Keep until you sell properties.)
- Burial lot deeds
- Car titles and bills of sale (Keep until you dispose of cars.)
- List of locations and numbers of bank accounts and investments
- Financial contracts, notes, and debts
- Government bond certificates

The Beauty of Binders

I'm sure I'm not the only one to use three-ring binders and clear plastic page protectors to organize all kinds of information. I have my recipes filed according to season in one binder and our household telephone list in another, and I'm using binders for my kids' scrapbooks, too. Binders are also great for keeping medical records like immunization dates handy. One woman I know made a reference sheet listing medical insurance numbers, doctors' names and phone numbers, emergency contacts, allergies, and other key information. She slipped it in a page protector and either left it out at home for baby sitters or brought it with her when she took her daughter elsewhere for child care.

Childproofing

It only takes seconds for curious children to get into things that can hurt them. The best way to keep kids safe is, of course, to keep a close eye on them. You can also prevent problems by making physical changes to your home. Following is a short list of childproofing tips I think are especially valuable for families with babies, toddlers, and preschoolers. But there are lots more important safety issues and great ideas to consider, and I encourage you to investigate them. (See the sidebar on page 155 for childproofing resources.)

Seven Smart Safety Strategies

1. Use plastic outlet protectors to keep little wet fingers away from electrical currents. They're incredibly cheap and easy to use.

2. Lock any cabinet or closet containing household cleaners, alcohol, medicines (including vitamins), toiletries, or other substances that may be toxic to kids.

3. Install safety locks on toilet lids, keep diaper pails tightly sealed if there's water in them, and never leave a young child unattended in the bathtub. Little kids can drown in less than an inch of water.

4. Never let kids play unsupervised around an electric garage door. Kids have died after getting pinned beneath closing doors. When you buy an electric door, get one with a sensor that stops its descent if any object or person is in the way.

5. If you have tables with sharp corners, move them, replace them, or attach safety bumpers.

6. If you have a yard where your child will be playing, fence it in. Your running into the house for even one minute to answer the phone or turn off the stove could give your kid a chance to escape from an unfenced yard.

7. Finally, while I think guns have no place in a home with children, I realize others feel differently. If you have guns in your home for sports or self-defense, take measures to reduce the chance of their causing accidental injury or death: Unload them, fit each with a safety lock, store them in a locked cabinet, and keep the ammunition in a separate location.

Handle with Care

If you have fragile treasures displayed within reach of little hands, consider packing them away for a few years to avoid breakage, even if it won't hurt anything but feelings. I've learned the hard way that a special glass stored in a cabinet within reach can be too tempting for a curious kid to resist. And I vividly recall my mother's dismay when my brother, who was throwing a ball around the living room, broke an exquisite chambered nautilus shell that my aunt had brought back from a trip to Kenya.

This is not to say that young children can't handle fragile items with supervision. In fact, early learning of proper handling techniques is not only possible but beneficial; it helps children hone their fine-motor skills and develop confidence in their abilities. But from day to day, it's probably best to keep the heirloom crystal out of reach.

Cleaning and Organizing

Division of Labor

Many at-home parents assume that because they're home during the day, housekeeping tasks like cleaning, cooking, laundry, and errands are part of their job description. "It just kind of happens," explains Heidi, a mom at home with her preschool-age son. "You feel like it's all your responsibility." This may be especially true for at-home moms, who find themselves in a very traditional female role laden with expectations.

Though some at-home parents enjoy being in control of their environment, others hate the assumption that in addition to all the daily parenting work they do, they must also get dinner on the table every night, face the breakfast dishes every morning, pick up the dry cleaning, shop for groceries, keep the house tidy, and so on. "It's exhausting," Heidi

Childproofing Resources

Web Sites

"Childproofing Your Home: 12 Safety Devices to Protect Your Children" by U.S. Consumer Product Safety Commission, http://www.cpsc.gov/cpscpub/pubs/grand/12steps/12steps.html

"Childproofing around the House" by BabyCenter.com, http://www.babycenter.com/refcap/baby/babysafety/460.html

Books

Baby Proofing Basics: How to Keep Your Child Safe, 2nd Edition by Vicki Lansky

On the Safe Side: Your Complete Reference to Childproofing for Infants and Toddlers by Cindy Wolf

Child Safe: A Practical Guide for Preventing Childhood Injuries Infancy to Age 14 by Mark A. Brandenburg, M.D.

says. "You really don't get a break." Cary agrees. "How do you, when you're the one at home, say, 'I'm done'?" She points out that it's much easier for someone who works outside the home to leave work behind, come home, and sit down to read the paper.

To avoid such tensions, many families ignore the expectations—traditional or otherwise—placed on at-home parents and simply divvy up household tasks in whatever way works best for them. Jane, who cares for her kids during the day and works part-time in the evenings and on weekends while Jim, her husband, does kid duty, says, "I'm not in a traditional role at all! I don't do housework. My husband is organized and does a lot of it. I think it's great for my kids to see my husband do the dishes or fold laundry."

According to an article on Slowlane.com, a web site by and for at-home dads, stay-at-home dads do as much cleaning, laundry, and cooking as stay-at-home moms. (On the weekends, though, at-home dads retain many of the maintenance jobs typically performed by men, such as lawn mowing and home repair.)[1]

Brian, an at-home father of two, says he's "not much of an indoor handyman," but otherwise his family's experience bears out the claims of the Slowlane article. "It's more of a partnership than with a traditional family," he says. "Susie comes home from work and takes some of the child-care role. First, she gets hugs and kisses all around, then plays with [the kids] while I get dinner ready. We tag-team on baths and bedtime. When we had just one kid, she did most of the bath-bedtime routine." Brian does the yard work and takes out the garbage. The two share laundry, dishes, and household upkeep. "It's a pretty good balance," Brian sums up.

Dave, another at-home dad with two teenage daughters, observes, "[My wife and I have] reversed a lot of traditional gender roles. I do traditional guy things like painting and cutting the grass, but also lots of dishes and laundry during the week. Part of the secret of our success is we're both willing to be rational about it. It's not reasonable to expect her to work forty hours a week [and come home to do the housework]. If she's going to work to bring in money, I have a responsibility to use my time productively at home."

There's no single housekeeping arrangement that works for every family, so it's important to communicate constantly about expectations and renegotiate chores when necessary. "It's good to talk about," says Cary.

"Set up systems to make household stuff run smoothly so those [tasks] aren't points of contention."

Who has access to a car? When does your child nap? Is an errand on the wage earner's way home? Could the laundry wait until evenings or Saturdays, when both parents are around? Think about issues like this as you assign chores.

Work Distribution Ideas

- Have the wage-earning partner take full responsibility for one or more household chores. Nanci's husband does the laundry, Kim's the dishes, and Kelly's the grocery shopping. Being freed up entirely from even one household responsibility can reduce a lot of stress for an at-home parent.

- Cook together on weekends. Freeze entire meals or make big pots of soup to last for a few days so cooking isn't a major undertaking every night of the week.

- Try on-line grocery shopping and delivery if it's available in your area. My family orders groceries from a service that delivers once a week. It's a bit more expensive than the discount supermarkets in our area, but it saves two hours a week. Sometimes time is more important than money.

- Hire someone to clean your home if you can afford it—even if it's only once a month or every other month. Coming home to a clean house is nice for everyone, not just the wage earner. Cary and her husband, Frank, have someone come in to clean once a month "as an egalitarian thing."

- Take turns doing various chores.

- As soon as your child is two or three years old, enlist his or her help with household tasks. (See pages 84–86 for a list of age-appropriate chores.)

- If you have more than one child, make a chore chart. This tool takes the burden off mom or dad to enforce responsibilities. It has really boosted cooperation among my kids—as long as I'm not too picky about how shiny the bathroom sink is or whether there's still some dog hair in the corners after the sweeping's done. I give lots of praise for hard work and issue gentle "suggestions" for next time.

Cleanliness Is Next to...

Finish this sentence with the noun or adjective of your choice. *Godliness?* I hope not. *Impossible?* It sure seems that way sometimes. I confess: Keeping a spotless house is not my strong suit. I like the idea of a clean house, but it's just not the most important thing in my daily life. Just in case cleanliness *is* next to godliness, though, I hope I'll score a few points in heaven for the following ideas, which I've picked up here and there on my journey as a stay-at-home mom.

General Cleaning and Clutter-Busting

The grit, grime, and clutter that take over your home when you have a child—crumbs on the couch, spit-up-stained clothing, sticky doorknobs, half-filled juice cups, stale bagels, neon-colored kid paraphernalia, small plastic toys that look harmless until you step on them with bare feet, baskets of unfolded laundry that sit for days—can be challenging to your personal aesthetics, especially when this is your home *and* your workplace. It can be overwhelming to even imagine tidying things up.

I think the real key to effective housekeeping when your family includes a child is to lower your expectations and cancel that subscription to *Metropolitan Home.* After you've come to terms with the idea of living in creative chaos, take a deep breath and consider the following suggestions:

- Try the old-fashioned one-day-at-a-time approach to housework: laundry Mondays, shopping Tuesdays, and so on. I never get past Tuesday, so I don't know what comes next. But if this system works for you, great!

- Tackle housecleaning one room at a time, starting with the dirtiest. Work from the farthest corner toward the door in each room.

- To make sure the important stuff gets done regularly without having to clean the whole house every week, try this strategy: Mop the kitchen floor, clean the bathroom, and vacuum weekly. Dust, clean the cupboards, clean the refrigerator, and so on monthly.

- Hire cleaning help if possible. Remember, though, that a housecleaner won't pick up clutter; you have to do that before he or she shows up.

- Store toys like Barbies, Legos, and art supplies in baskets or in clear plastic containers with lids. (Baskets are easy to find at garage sales, and inexpensive plastic containers are available at most discount stores.) You can stack these on the floor, line them up on shelves, store them in a closet, or slide them under a bed.

- Set aside a couple of baskets for tossing things you don't want to deal with right away. Go through them every so often to file, recycle, put away, and so on.

- Declare one room in your house—perhaps your bedroom or office—off-limits to your child. Close the door. This is your haven.

- Train your child at a young age to put away toys or materials he or she has been using before taking out the next batch.

- Close your child's bedroom door if his or her junk bugs you.

- Have a daily ten-minute pickup session after lunch, before dinner, before bed, or whenever you think you need it most.

Keeping Kids Healthy

One of the best things about having a parent at home is avoiding the annoying recurrent bouts with colds, flu, strep throat, and other illnesses that kids tend to pick up at daycare. And the ability to be with your child when he or she does get sick brings great peace of mind. But even if you can stay home when your child is ill, preventing illness is the first priority. Here are a few tips on staying germ-free:

- Wash your bathroom and kitchen towels frequently. I change mine every single day. Maybe I'm a fanatic, but I figure it can't hurt!

- If you use sponges or scouring pads to wash your dishes, replace them or run them through the dishwasher often.

- Sterilize bottle parts, baby spoons, pacifiers, and breast pump parts by immersing them in boiling water for a few minutes, running them through the dishwasher on the highest-heat cycle, or using a microwave or electric steam sterilizer.

- Toothbrushes are notorious germ magnets. Run them through the dishwasher once in a while or invest a few bucks in new toothbrushes every couple of months. To save money and waste, buy toothbrushes with replaceable heads (available at many natural foods stores).

- Encourage everyone in your family to wash his or her hands often—especially before eating or preparing food and after diaper changing and using the bathroom. Keep an alcohol-based hand sanitizer in your diaper bag or purse at all times.

- Baby wipes are not just for babies anymore. They're great for all kinds of cleanup in the car, in the kitchen, and of course, in the bathroom or at the changing table.

- Avoid antibacterial soaps and cleaning products. Plain old hot, soapy water or alcohol-based products kill bacteria just as well without contributing to the problem of resistant bacteria.

The Diaper Debate

When it comes to cleanliness, few issues are as onerous—and certainly none as odorous—as diapers. This is not the place for the definitive debate on cloth versus disposable, but let's take a quick look at the advantages and disadvantages of both options. (See the table on page 161.) For all the advice and information you could ever want about cloth diapering, hop online and visit http://www.borntolove.com. For information and advice on both cloth and disposable diapering, visit http://www.drspock.com and/or http://kidshealth.org and search using the keyword *diapering*.

Useful Equipment

Here's a list of tried-and-true equipment that makes an active life with a child easier to manage. You can get many of these items at resale stores or garage sales. If you have or plan to have more than one child, you might want to invest in new stuff that will last.

Baby Gear

- *Highchair:* If you have a spacious dining area, a full-size highchair is probably your best bet. If space is tight, a booster seat (with or without a tray) works well. You could also try a seat that clamps directly onto the table—but note that this type of seat can be used on sturdy, four-legged tables only.

- *Car seat:* This is one place not to skimp. A hand-me-down may or may not meet current safety standards. Get a manual to go with your seat and call the manufacturer to check product recalls. Also,

Diaper Comparison

	Conventional Disposables	Cotton Diapers
Convenience	Easy to use. Fitted design helps prevent leaks. Can be tossed in any garbage receptacle. Must be emptied into toilet before disposal, though few users do this. Must be purchased regularly. Most daycare providers insist on disposables. Very absorbent	Easy to use new Velcro and snap designs. (No pins needed.) Must be used with moisture-resistant covers. Fitted designs help prevent leaks. Must be washed either at home or by diaper service. Must be emptied into toilet before washing. Must be stored until washed. Few daycare providers will use cloth. Less absorbent.
Cost	More expensive option.	Less expensive option if washing at home. Cost varies if using diaper service, but is usually comparable to or slightly less than disposables.
Environmental impact	Require large amounts of wood, plastics, energy, and water to manufacture. Manufacturing releases pollutants into environment. Fill up landfills and take hundreds of years to decompose. Leach chemicals into groundwater from landfills. Leach raw sewage into groundwater because few users empty into toilet before tossing.	Require fewer natural resources to manufacture. Are reusable. Require water and energy to wash, but less than used in manufacture of disposables. Require multiple washings and use of bleach if washed by diaper service. If washed at home, require no toxic chemicals (phosphates, bleach, and so on). Do not fill up landfills or contaminate groundwater.
Health	Contain sodium polyacrylate for absorbency, which is linked to toxic shock syndrome. Contain carcinogenic dioxin as a byproduct of bleaching. High absorbency may tempt users to leave dirty diapers on too long. Infrequent changes, perfumes, and other chemicals may contribute to diaper rash and allergic reactions.	Can be washed without leaving chemical residues that come into contact with baby's skin. Less absorbent material encourages more frequent changing, which may reduce diaper rash.
Comfort	High absorbency means baby feels drier. Paper product isn't as soft against baby's skin as cotton. Plastic outer covering does not breathe and traps heat.	Less absorbent material means baby feels wet when diaper is dirty. Wet feeling may encourage earlier toilet learning. Cotton is softer against baby's skin than paper products. Fabric diapers and covers breathe, helping baby stay cool.

make sure you install the seat properly, or it may not protect your precious cargo in the event of an accident. The Child Passenger Safety page of the National Highway Traffic Safety Administration's web site (http://www. nhtsa.dot.gov/people/injury/childps) provides excellent information on buying, installing, and using car seats and

Baby Walkers

Baby walkers, though popular, are largely discredited by child development and safety experts. Not only do they *not* help a child learn to walk, they're dangerous because they can roll down stairs in a nanosecond—even when a parent or other adult is present—posing great risk of injury to children. The American Academy of Pediatrics (AAP) says baby walker injuries sent 20,100 children to the hospital emergency room in 1995 and that they caused the death of thirty-four children between 1973 and 1998.

The AAP has backed a ban on baby walkers, claiming that their use disrupts children's ability to develop walking and visual skills and stops them from properly exploring their surroundings. The AAP suggests parents throw out their baby walkers and refuse to leave their children in any home or daycare facility that uses walkers.

Source: "Injuries Associated with Infant Walkers," a policy statement reported in *Pediatrics,* 108:3 (September 2001): pp. 790–92.

makes it easy for parents to keep up-to-date on U.S. child passenger safety laws and product recalls.

- *Bouncy seat:* In my house, a "bouncy seat" is a soft cloth seat on a low, angled frame with a safety strap to hold baby in. It's handy for infants who can't sit up yet, as it props them up a bit so they can see what's going on around them. When you're making dinner or taking a shower, you can tote baby right along. A car seat can serve the same purpose, but a bouncy seat may be more comfortable and less confining. My sister-in-law keeps one on each floor of her house.

- *Baby carrier:* Across centuries, cultures, and continents, parents have toted their kids everywhere by using slings, backpacks, and other hands-free carriers. Find the type that suits you best before you buy by trying various models in a store (bring a baby or a doll along to help you test them) or borrowing from friends. Whatever type of carrier you choose, make sure you can put it on and take it off easily. One friend of mine says carrying her babies in a sling on walks and outings was much more comfortable for her than pushing a stroller. As her babies grew, she switched to a backpack, which allowed her and her husband to bring them on cross-country ski outings.

- *Full-size stroller:* You'll want this for everyday walks, shopping trips, and other outings. It should provide a comfy ride for your kid, safety straps, a canopy to keep the sun or rain off, and plenty of storage space. I also recommend investing in some stroller netting to keep the bugs off your little one when you're outdoors.

- *Compact stroller:* This type of stroller is sometimes called an umbrella stroller because of its hooked handles. Whatever you call it, it's lightweight and folds up quite small. It's a lifesaver for air travel because even with moving sidewalks, airport terminals require lots of walking. Some compact strollers can be stowed in overhead compartments on airplanes. A compact stroller is also handy if you use public transportation or live in an upstairs apartment.

- *Jogging stroller:* A jogger is essential for taking baby along if you're a runner or in-line skater. It also makes a good all-terrain vehicle for hikes on unpaved trails.

- *Bike trailer or baby seat:* If biking is your thing, you'll want to bring baby along! (And what kid doesn't enjoy whizzing around town like royalty in a private chariot?)

- *Playpen or portable crib:* While some parents don't like the thought of fencing in their children, others believe judicious use of a playpen or portable crib keeps babies safe and within sight when it's time to make dinner or tend to another child. A portable crib is especially handy for traveling and/or keeping at grandma and grandpa's house.

- *Safety locks, latches, and covers:* There are lots of devices you can install on cupboards, drawers, doors, faucets, toilets, outlets, lids, and other household fixtures to keep active, curious tykes out of harm's way. See pages 153–55 for more childproofing information.

Big-Kid Stuff

- *Add-on bike:* This contraption attaches to the back of an adult bike. It looks like a tandem bicycle with a kid-size caboose. It's great for kids who are comfortable on two wheels but can't quite keep up with parents and older siblings on long bike rides.

- *Bike helmets:* These are absolutely essential for biking safety. Everyone in the family should wear one, no matter how goofy you may think they look!

Sippy Cups

Sippy cups are by no means lethal, but they may contribute significantly to tooth decay—especially the ones with lids that have a valve that requires a child to suck rather than sip and swallow. "It's the amount of time liquid stays in the mouth" that contributes to cavities, says dentist and mom of three Kordie Reinhold. She goes on to explain that prolonged use of sippy cups may slow a child's development of drinking and even speech. "Those things are interrelated in subtle ways," says Reinhold.

A better alternative is a cup with a lid and collapsible straw or a sippy cup with a simple, valveless lid. Avoid sweetened juices and soft drinks and opt for water or unsweetened juices instead. "Use cups with lids for the car or the stroller," suggests Reinhold, "but don't stop trying to show kids how to drink from a regular cup without a lid."

- *Back yard play structure:* This one's pricey, but probably worth it. If you don't live near a playground and/or it's not safe for your kids to walk to the local playground alone, you'll reap rich rewards in kid-hours of outdoor play logged from a good back yard play structure. You can buy one ready to assemble or design and build your own. Avoid brands made of wood treated with arsenic, which is dangerous for both humans and pets.

- *Kiddie pool or sprinkler:* On a hot day there's nothing better than sending your kid outside in a swimsuit to get soaked! You must supervise your child when he or she is in or near any pool—no matter how small—but kids can run through a sprinkler on their own. A good old-fashioned garden sprinkler works fine, but there are lots of kid-oriented water gadgets out there, too. All you need to do is supply dry towels and Popsicles afterward.

- *Backpack:* This is essential for school and also comes in handy on day trips to the museum, the beach, and on hikes and bike rides. Giving children backpacks may help them take responsibility for hauling their own stuff. It won't completely stop the parent-as-repository syndrome—you know, when your kid says, "Here, hold this," while shoving a note from the teacher, lunch box, musical instrument, or jacket at you while making a running start for the playground—but it's a start.

- *Outdoor sports equipment:* Bikes, sleds, basketballs and nets, ice skates, in-line skates, and other such stuff enhances opportunities for family fun and exercise.

- *Musical instrument:* Music is part of a well-rounded education. You can rent a band instrument if you're not sure the trombone will take or the flutist will flourish.

- *Personal CD player:* One player per child can cure the headaches caused by competing musical tastes and long car rides.

- *Cell phone:* Some parents of preteens and teens feel great peace of mind knowing they can communicate with their children anytime, anywhere. To avoid running up a huge bill, establish rules of use with your child.

- *Library card:* This little item opens more doors than anything else on this list—and it's a freebie!

Chapter 6

Everything Changes

Even if you've had the most blissful at-home experience, there will likely come a time when you return to the paid work force. Maybe your partner loses his or her job or becomes disabled or ill. Your child heads off to first grade or college. You get the job offer of your dreams. Your partner wants a turn to stay home. Your leave of absence from employment ends. You're itchy to get back in the marketplace. You've discovered a new career. Whatever your reason(s), you realize it's time to make a change.

Preparing for Reemployment

Defining Your Goals

Your reasons for reentering the job market may affect the type of employment you seek. Before you start looking for a job, it's a good idea to define your reemployment goals. Most at-home parents in transition fall into one of these three categories:

- *Downshifting:* Folks in this category are seeking jobs (often part-time) that permit them to spend most of their time with their families. Their at-home experiences may have changed their views about work-family balance. They may want jobs in their fields that use their experience but offer less stress and greater flexibility with home life than their previous jobs did.

- *Now where was I?* Job seekers in this category are hoping to pick up their careers where they left off. The fewer years they've been out of the job market and the more they've maintained their professional connections, the easier this is.

● *Branching out:* Sometimes parenting or the break from employment stimulates an entrepreneurial spirit or a new area of interest. This option often requires retraining or repackaging oneself.

Work-Family Balance

Many parents in North America feel the tug of two strong forces on their psyches. In our culture, a job often is not just what pays the grocery bill, but also what defines us in shorthand for other people and what gives us a sense of purpose in life. It's natural for any adult to want to get out there, mix it up with other adults, and make an impact on the marketplace. But many parents also realize that balancing paid work with family work is of key importance. That's why a lot of at-home parents returning to employment don't end up with traditional full-time jobs.

Some parents who've been at home during their children's early years find that the way their kids need them changes as the kids grow older, but the need for parental presence remains. School-age children and teenagers can care for themselves physically in many ways: They can fix their own snacks and meals, do household chores, get themselves safely to and from school, even stay home alone for a while. But they also have needs that may not be immediately evident: to talk at the drop of a hat, to be with people who love them unconditionally, to revert to being children after a day of trying to hold it all together in front of teachers and peers.

Mary is a certified public accountant who stayed home with her children for a year and a half, then began part time work as a bookkeeper at a food cooperative, a job well below her professional capabilities but suited to her priorities. Her weekly schedule included mostly evenings and just one day shift, so she only needed child care one day a week, and she could walk to work. "Getting my foot back in the door was really a positive thing," Mary says. "It also helped me identify what's important to me in a job. Having kids completely reversed my feelings about that." The bookkeeping job led to a better-paid job at a larger co-op that also gave her a 15-percent discount on groceries.

Now Mary works eighteen to twenty-five hours a week as the accountant for a publishing services company. She has a fixed workload but by and large sets her own schedule. She says she'll probably return to full-time work someday, but at the moment her family's needs take priority, especially now that her children are in middle school and high school. Mary considers these vulnerable years; she's seen family friends in serious crises as their adolescent children have struggled with drug and alcohol use, running away, and mental illness. "I think it's really important for me to be there when they come home from school," she says, "so they're not alone. I can try to make sure they're doing safe things and making good choices."

Maggie is another mom carefully balancing family and career decisions. Formerly a social worker and an elementary school teacher, she stayed home with her two children for four years, then felt the need to re-ignite her professional life. She eased into part-time work in adult basic education and eventually began teaching English to adult immigrants.

She loves her students and her work but has struggled with her schedule. Many of her classes are on weekends and evenings to accommodate the needs of working adults. "I was talking with another mother at work," she says. "We agree that it's still really important to be with our kids even though they're older. My kids are great. They tell me, 'It's not your responsibility to make dinner every night.' But I missed connecting with them." Maggie had been working four nights a week, but she cut back to two.

Reinventing Yourself

Many at-home parents switch gears careerwise because they've clarified their values, learned new skills, developed new interests, or observed market niches they hadn't noticed before kids. Volunteering or taking classes can also spark new ideas about where to focus one's energy and time. Some parents return to the career dreams they'd had in younger days. For example, Linda, a lawyer, says that in college she'd been interested in medicine and has considered returning to school to become a physician's assistant. Heidi says she's always wanted to be a nurse and probably won't go back into the computer field.

Staying in the Loop

Vicki Bacal, a career coach, consultant, and résumé writer since 1985 whose work has been published in *Resumes! Resumes! Resumes!*, insists that at-home parents "have a plan for the long haul." She says it's great to stay home with your kids if that's your priority, but "have a backup plan. Keep your irons in the fire."

Career counselor Colleen Convey observes that many people who've been out of the work force for a while face mental roadblocks as they start their career reentry efforts. They tend to "feel so out of it," she explains. For this ailment, an ounce of prevention is worth a pound of cure.

Be Visible

Convey says at-home parents "don't have to do a ton, just a little bit. They will feel more confident and they will be more up-to-date." She recommends, "Keep visible during that time away. Stay active in an organization, go to meetings, volunteer to be on the membership committee—so you're still part of the community."

Maintaining relationships with former colleagues can tip you off to new opportunities, provide references, and help you stay on top of trends. Keeping in touch is fairly easy, but it does require conscientious effort. Make regular phone calls to former colleagues to catch up on office gossip and industry news. Take advantage of social opportunities to get some face time with former coworkers, customers, and competitors.

Even if you suppressed a gleeful grin as you walked away from your job and toward at-home parenthood, don't burn your bridges, advises Bacal. Regardless of whether you intend to return to the same field, you'll need professional references someday—preferably ones who'll smile when they hear your name, glad to share glowing reports about you with prospective employers. "Carve yourself a path so you can get back if you need to," Bacal says. "Don't allow a door to close if you might want to go back in, even if it's ten years later."

Kim, a lawyer, stayed visible during her at-home years not only by staying connected to her old professional life, but also by reaching forward into her future one. She knew her time at home was limited, because she and her husband wanted to send their children to private school and needed her salary to pay tuition. She also missed "the security of having an income and outside adults who reinforce your sense of worth." For her, the question was never *whether* to resume her career, but *when*. "I interviewed for jobs on and off the whole time I was home," she says. A relationship she developed through this process turned into a phone call and a near-perfect job offer when she was finally ready to go back. She now works 80 percent–time, which lets her pick up her kids from school and spend time with them afterward.

Kim's experience hammers home the importance of networking. Statisticians and job counselors agree that the majority of jobs are found this way. For every job advertised, there are two or three other openings you don't hear about unless you know people who belong to or are involved with the organizations in question. Obviously, you have a much better chance of landing one of those jobs if you know it exists and you're well connected!

Keep Current

You know how valuable your time at home has been—how it's changed you, what you've learned, what extraordinary patience, time management, and problem-solving skills you've developed—and perhaps a prospective employer will understand your employment history in the context of the important effort to balance family and work. Unfortunately, it's far more likely that whoever's hiring will see a break in a résumé as a red flag.

Alex, father of two daughters, recalls searching for a job during his stint at home. From that experience he learned the hard truth that "home time is practically worthless in most employers' eyes if you've done nothing else." In other words, it's important not only to stay visible, but also to stay current—to actively improve yourself, just as you would if you were employed.

Networking

For loads of practical and entertaining advice on networking—basic instructions, tips for special situations, how to schmooze if you hate to schmooze, gaffes to avoid, and more—visit http://networking.monster.com/archives.

Strategies for Staying Employable

Just because most of your brain cells are busy with the minutiae of making kids happy and managing your household doesn't mean you can't hold a few in reserve for your "other life." Here are some ways to do that:

- Keep up with contacts and reading in your field so you're aware of anything coming down the pike, such as new technology, marketing trends, products, services, or research.
- Send holiday cards to former clients and coworkers. You never know when you'll need a reference, and you want to make sure you're still in their Rolodexes.
- Take a class to update your technology skills.
- Maintain licensure or certification if you're in a field such as teaching, social work, human resources, psychology, nursing, and so on.
- Assume volunteer leadership roles that help you make connections while contributing to a good cause and bolstering your résumé.
- Put in ten hours a week doing productive work outside your home sphere. (Adjust this to your reality—if you can manage only a half-day each week, take it and run with it!)
- Line up references from a particular job or volunteer position while you're still working at it.
- Network. You needn't be a social menace; just keep in mind that every single person you know is a potential job lead.

If you're reentering the work force under duress—perhaps you're newly divorced, mourning the death of your partner, or dealing with an unexpected job loss—it's going to be even more difficult emotionally than if the change were your choice. And if you're not ready to jump into a job that could pay your bills, your stress will be infinitely compounded, says Bacal. She's witnessed the sad effects of sudden widowhood on close friends. She also knows a couple who depleted their savings when the husband lost his job and even a year and a half later the wife couldn't generate adequate income to cover their bills.

That's why Bacal is adamant that stay-at-home parents set aside ten hours a week for volunteering, paid work, or education that can be written on a résumé. (Like it or not, that piece of paper is still really important.) And she insists that every at-home parent have a reemployment plan. "I see women not planning and then being very sad, very upset that nobody wants them. If they keep [themselves marketable]," Bacal says, "they can do both"—that is, have successful at-home *and* reemployment experiences.

Pounding the Pavement
Job Hunting Tips

Word of mouth is the best way to start any job search and ultimately the most likely to result in interviews or offers. When you're ready to reenter the job market, tell everyone you know that you're actively looking. (Here's where keeping those connections will pay off.)

Be yourself in interviews, but "do not sit around and talk about your kids!" advises Bacal. On the flip side, neither should you apologize for the "gap" in your résumé. Ann Crittenden, author of *The Price of Motherhood*, actually advises that you include your parenting experience on your résumé, both to validate the work you've done as "real" work with measurable value and to show you have indeed gained worthwhile insights and learned or honed transferable skills. Management and communication are obvious areas of development. Many at-home parents report that their efficiency at all kinds of work increases due to the habit of multitasking. Others note that taking a break from employment helps them return with a valuable outsider's perspective.

I figure that if an employer is wary of your decision to take yourself out of the market to raise your child, you might want to think twice about working for an organization with that ethos. If someone asks what you've been doing with yourself for the past few years, be honest. Say, "I made a choice to be with my kid, and I don't regret it."

Be sure to include family friendliness in your job search criteria. For example, does a prospective employer offer flex time, job sharing, on-site child care, sick days, and/or a decent vacation package? Don't just rely on the written company policies or annual ratings by national magazines; talk to employees or former employees to find out the real scoop.

Be Realistic

Convey notes that the average job search is six to nine months, even for someone who's looking for a job in the same field as the last job he or she held. "If people don't have realistic expectations," she says, "they can get discouraged really fast. They can start to think negatively about their skills."

Robert Frank, a psychologist who has studied at-home dads, notes that the trend of dads staying home is still new enough that many have yet to face career reentry; they're still home with their four- and five-year-old children. "Most say they want to get the first five years [of their children's lives], or three years or whatever it is, out of the way," Frank says, "then they'll think about their careers again."

Career counselors agree that a transitional job can help build the confidence of someone who's been out of the market for a long time. Bacal, for example, had a client who wanted to get back to work in marketing after being home for ten years with two children and a case

A Pro at Work: Smart Résumé Writing

One mother, previously a human resources manager, had been home for several years with two children with time consuming special needs, says Vicki Bacal. While still at home, she hired a baby sitter so she could pursue current certification. "We put that education front and center on the résumé," says Bacal. "Here she is totally updated, not over the hill, not stale, not needing training."

The same woman had also co-chaired several committees and events at her church, at her children's school, and in her community. Bacal advised downplaying the children's issues and the specific church, since those weren't the focus of her client's job search, and instead listing the volunteer work under "Fundraising Committees."

of severe depression. "She had graduated very high in her class in marketing," Bacal says, and she'd once directed a whole group of sales representatives, but she'd only taken small jobs since then. Working with Bacal, she landed a job selling subscriptions for her local daily newspaper's advertising department. "She left [the work force] making fifty thousand dollars a year, and she's now making eleven dollars an hour. But already after several months she is now an insider who knows there is a job opening up for a supervisor."

When to Hire a Pro

If you're at a loss about where to start, hire a professional to help you package yourself. A career counselor will look at what you've done, listen to where you want to go, and help you come up with tools and strategies to get you there. He or she will help you make the most of your existing connections and probably come up with a few new ones, too.

If you find yourself reentering the work force under adverse circumstances, such as a family financial crisis or your partner's sudden illness or job loss, a career counselor may provide just the support you need to get you on your feet and into the marketplace. "Some people intend not to go back [to work], and then things change," says Convey. "You have to give up a dream and deal with the loss before you move on to the new."

After You've Found That Perfect Job

Finding Child Care

For many stay-at-home parents, finding high-quality, affordable child care is the most difficult aspect of reentering the marketplace. There are lots of options, and choosing the right one for your family will take some work.

Ask people you know to recommend good providers. Call your local daycare association for a member list. If you're looking for someone to provide care in your home, call nanny agencies. Visit daycare providers or interview nannies to assess the fit for your family. Consider quality of care, first of all. Look for a provider with good credentials or certification who behaves in a professional manner with you and is warm and caring with your child. Then check out hours of operation, policies, location, and cost.

If your child is school-age, child care may not seem as big a concern as it would if he or she were younger. But keep in mind that school-age children lacking adequate after-school supervision may be at greater risk for getting into trouble because they are bored and lonely. That's why it's very important to make arrangements for their care.

While it might be okay to allow a responsible child of ten or older to occasionally spend a short time alone before a parent comes home, it's probably not a good idea to make it a daily routine. Even if a child exhibits good judgment and maturity, he or she may not be emotionally ready to be in charge for any length of time and should not be pressured to do so—especially if a younger sibling is home, too.

Check out your local schools and community organizations for after-school programs. Consider hiring a teenager or college student to baby-sit after school. Arrange your work schedule so you can be home when your child gets home. Or trade before- and after-school care with another family—for example, if your child can go to their house after school, theirs can come to yours before school or on weekends.

Adjusting to Working outside the Home

Your new life as a gainfully employed parent will require some adjustment. You'll probably have to squeeze more time with your child into fewer hours, and you'll have to prioritize other commitments and social opportunities—perhaps even eliminate some. You and your child and spouse may have to redistribute household work, with everyone taking on more equal responsibility. You'll probably have some anxiety about daycare. You might be more tired at the end of the day.

On the other hand, you'll surely find that employment has its benefits, too. You may have more income to pay someone else to clean your house or mow your lawn. You might be able to go out to eat more often, take a great family vacation, and/or bolster your retirement or college savings. And best of all, you'll probably be happier than ever to see your kids after a day apart.

Afterword

A Society in Search of Balance

Parents who spend any period of their children's lives at home full-time are bound to question their decision occasionally.

Emotionally, we want work that makes us feel as if we're contributing to our society, whether we're cashiers or chefs, bus drivers or biology teachers, artists or aerospace engineers. We don't necessarily get this feeling day in and day out with children, who often try our patience and tax our inner resources.

Speaking of taxing.... Financially, we also want work that enables us to keep roofs over our heads, put peanut butter sandwiches in lunch boxes, and visit grandma and grandpa once or twice a year.

As we grapple with the emotional and material challenges of at-home parenting, many of us wonder: Why is the work of parenting and household management given so much lip service and so little real respect? Why is it so hard to make ends meet with a parent at home during our children's most needy formative years? Where's the work-family balance in our society?

Our culture has evolved to support a division of labor. Public labor is work that's paid, taxed, and included in our gross national product (GNP), the total value of all goods and services produced in our economy. Private labor, or that which is not paid, taxed, or counted in the GNP, includes the work of parents raising children and managing households. So if I hire a maid to clean my bathroom, it counts as something measurably productive in our national economy because it has a wage attached to it. If I clean my bathroom myself, it doesn't count. And I'll never see a social security check generated by it.

Social scientists have calculated a hypothetical market value of about thirty-five thousand dollars a year for the work of an at-home parent based on a job description including the typical responsibilities of a person in that position, like cleaning, laundry, chauffeuring, cooking, and child care. Ann Crittenden's book *The Price of Motherhood* details the social and economic hardships at-home parents experience and suggests that solutions must include changes in our economic policies and corporate and government practices about family leave, taxation, and retirement benefits.

Of course, what isn't counted in this discussion is the part of at-home parenting that doesn't translate easily into hard data. The quality of life for a child with a parent at home may be enhanced, but the value of that is hard to measure. It isn't fashionable or politically correct to say that at-home parents make a big contribution to our society in the long run because they improve their families' emotional well-being. But I wonder about the societal costs of children who don't have people watching over them—people very like parents, who care deeply about who the children are, what they dream for their lives, what they fear—who have known them longer and better than anyone. Will children who lack such anchors end up like unmoored boats—bobbing along, drifting, maybe okay in the long run, or maybe capsizing in the end?

Where We've Been

Ironically, our next step forward may be a step backward. Recent trends toward home-based employment and sequencing of parenting and employment hearken back to the colonial American model of balancing public and private activities.

Then, women were largely responsible for the economic as well as the parenting interests of the family. Weaving, spinning, and other trades were performed by households and were managed by the women who ran those households. Domestic work was usually done by unmarried young women to free married women for work in family industries. "In effect," writes Madonna Kolbenschlag in *Kiss Sleeping Beauty Goodbye*, "women of the colonial era were not forced to choose between work and domesticity."

Kolbenschlag explains that as the American economy became industrialized, women's power and status decreased. The family enterprises they had run successfully died out as large factories, owned and operated by men, replaced them. Women were left with child rearing and household management. The public, or paid, industrial sphere of activity and the private, or unpaid, domestic sphere of activity became separated.

Women came to be seen as properly relegated to the quiet domesticity of home and hearth. In fact, women were put on a pedestal by the cultish Victorian ideal of "true womanhood," which also equated leisure (available only to the wealthy) with moral superiority and work with disgrace. Manual labor like cleaning and factory work became more dehumanizing. Workers doing these jobs had a hard time making decent wages and supporting their families.

Women and men are still paying the debt incurred by accepting this bill of goods. In reaction to the societal imbalance, our work habits have flip-flopped: We still accept the separation of public and private labor, only today women are as likely as men to be consumed by complete dedication to the public sphere. This upwardly mobile work ethic is just as dehumanizing as the industrial age's oppression of poor factory workers.

The Road We're On

I think it's a healthy sign that this ethic has been called into question by prominent women like Governor Jane Swift of Massachusetts. Swift quit her reelection bid because, as she said in a *New York Times* article, "Something had to give. I am sure there isn't a working parent in America that hasn't faced it, that when the demands of two tasks you take on both increase substantially, something has to give."

Mothers and fathers in similar situations are on the parenting interstate—they're forced to take the fastest route from birth to college. Life is focused on the next rest stop, the McDonald's oasis, the state line. There's no time for the unexpected roadside restaurants, funky museums, and little-visited historic sites that make the trip worth taking.

Destination Home

Today, a parent who works at home is likely to be running an information-based cottage industry from a home computer while the kids are napping, in school, or with an in-house baby sitter. The workload is tailored to the family's needs, not vice versa. Sometimes business and family needs overlap and require some juggling, but this kind of arrangement often provides the flexibility and freedom a parent needs in order to feel fulfillment in both public and private work.

However, home-based work rarely provides the financial stability a family requires to keep themselves housed, fed, clothed, and medically insured. And the quality of care received by children of work-at-home parents is another issue worth investigating. We know a great deal more about the psychological, cognitive, and spiritual development of our children than ever before, and parents perceive more than ever how great the responsibility of parenthood truly is. Therefore, the issues for twenty-first-century families are even more complex than they were for seventeenth- or eighteenth-century families.

For now, individual families must do the best they can with what they have. The vast majority of families who decide to have a parent at home are not wealthy. They're middle-class wage earners who believe that the best person to raise a child is that child's parent. They have serious questions about the quality of daycare. They're willing to put up with the uncertainty of leaving the work force because they want to do the parenting themselves. They don't want to take the interstate through their children's childhood, they want to get off on those two-lane roads that take you through interesting stops and make for better memories and stories.

By choosing to spend more time with their children, these parents will learn not only about who their children are, but probably something more about themselves. Parenting can teach a person new skills, greater compassion, and a healthy respect for boundaries and limitations. Parenting is humbling and important work. It's also empowering and equalizing—people across class, race, religious, and gender lines are seeking ways to be the best parents they can be. The good news is that there are more choices than ever about who will stay home, for how long, and under what conditions—and this book, I hope, serves as a road map for those who want to take the scenic route through their children's growing-up years.

Recommended Resources

Motherhood and Parenthood

Clarke, Jean Illsley. *Self-Esteem: A Family Affair*. Hazelden Information & Educational Services.

Doherty, William J. *Take Back Your Kids: Confident Parenting in Turbulent Times*. Sorin Books.

————. *Take Back Your Marriage: Sticking Together in a World That Pulls Us Apart*. Guilford Press.

Hrdy, Sarah Blaffer. *Mother Nature: A History of Mothers, Infants, and Natural Selection*. Pantheon Books.

Kabat-Zinn, Myla, and Jon Kabat-Zinn. *Everyday Blessings: The Inner Work of Mindful Parenting*. Hyperion Press.

Kolbenschlag, Madonna. *Kiss Sleeping Beauty Goodbye: Breaking the Spell of Feminine Myths and Models*. HarperCollins.

On-line Resources

Childbirth and Postpartum Professional Association, http://www.labordoula.com.

Main Street Mom, http://www.mainstreetmom.com.

Magazines

Brain, Child: The Magazine for Thinking Mothers

Other Media Resources

MOMbo: A Radio Resource for Moms

Work-Family Balance

Cardozo, Arlene Rossen. *Sequencing*. Brownstone.

Crittenden, Ann. *The Price of Motherhood: Why the Most Important Job in the World Is Still the Least Valued*. Owl Books.

Hayden, Ruth L. *For Richer, Not Poorer: The Money Book for Couples*. Health Communications.

Topolnicki, Denise M. *How to Raise a Family on Less than Two Incomes: The Complete Guide to Managing Your Money Better So You Can Spend More Time with Your Kids*. Broadway Books.

On-line Resources

Crown Financial Ministries, http://www.crown.org/tools/mommake.asp.

Dollar Stretcher, http://www.stretcher.com/index.cfm.

Family and Home Network, http://www.familyandhome.org.

Hearts at Home, http://www.hearts-at-home.org.

Mocha Moms, http://www.mochamoms.org.

Mothers & More, http://www.mothersandmore.org.

National Association for the Self-Employed, http://www.nase.org.

National Association of At-Home Mothers, http://www.athomemothers.com.

National Association of Entrepreneurial Parents, http://www.en-parent.com/index.htm.

Slowlane, http://www.slowlane.com.

Work at Home Moms, http://www.wahm.com.

Work Options, http://www.workoptions.com.

Job-Hunters Bible, http://www.jobhuntersbible.com.

Child Care and Development

Ames, Louise Bates, et al. Gesell Institute Child Development series. DTP.

Brazelton, T. Berry, M.D. *Infants and Mothers: Differences in Development*. Delacorte Press.

Dreikurs, Rudolf, M.D. *Children: The Challenge*. Plume.

———. *Discipline Without Tears*. Plume.

Field, Christine M. *Life Skills for Kids: Equipping Your Child for the Real World*. Harold Shaw.

Leach, Penelope. *Babyhood: Stage by Stage, from Birth to Age Two; How Your Baby Develops Physically, Emotionally, Mentally*. Knopf.

———. *Children First: What Society Must Do—And Is Not Doing—for Children Today*. Random House Trade Paperbacks.

———. *Your Baby and Child: From Birth to Age Five*. Knopf.

———. *Your Growing Child*. Random House Trade Paperbacks.

Montessori, Maria. *The Absorbent Mind*. Henry Holt.

———. *The Secret of Childhood*. Ballantine Books.

Sears, William, M.D., and Martha Sears, R.N. *The Attachment Parenting Book: A Commonsense Guide to Understanding and Nurturing Your Baby*. Little Brown & Co.

On-line Resources

Doulas of North America, http://www.dona.org.

I Am Your Child Foundation, http://www.iamyourchild.org.

La Leche League, http://www.lalecheleague.org.

National Parent Information Network, http://www.npin.org.

Parent Advocacy Coalition for Educational Rights (PACER), http://www.pacer.org.

Screen It!: Entertainment Reviews, http://www.screenit.com.

Magazines

Mothering

Parenting

Other Media Resources

Public Broadcasting Station

Cooking

Chalmers, Irena. *The Working Family's Cookbook*. Barron's Educational Series, Inc.

Karmel, Annabel. *First Meals: Fast, Healthy, and Fun Foods to Tempt Infants and Toddlers from Baby's First Foods to Favorite Family Feasts*. Dorling Kindersley Publishing.

Longacre, Doris Janzen *More-with-Less Cookbook*. Herald Press.

Working Mother magazine. *Working Mother Cookbook: Easy, Delicious Recipes and Time-Saving Techniques*. St Martin's Griffin.

References

Chapter 1

1. Cf. Sarah Blaffer Hrdy's *Mother Nature.*
2. Jacqueline Jones, *Labor of Love, Labor of Sorrow: Black Women, Work, and the Family, from Slavery to the Present,* Vintage Books (1985): pp. 155–65.
3. Tracey A. Reeves, "Trading Suits for Sweats: Black Moms Unite Against Pressures to Return to Their Jobs," *Washington Post Sunday* (November 12, 2000): p. C01.
4. Mai Weismantle, *Reasons People Do Not Work: 1996,* Current Population Reports, U.S. Census Bureau, Washington, DC (2001): pp. 70–76.
5. "Breastfeeding and the Use of Human Milk," policy statement reported in *Pediatrics,* 100:6 (December 1997): p. 1035.
6. Child Trends, *Charting Parenthood 2002: A Statistical Portrait of Fathers and Mothers in America.*
7. Robert Frank, telephone interview, (February 13, 2002).
8. Kristin Smith, telephone interview, (March 24, 2002).
9. Robert Frank, "Research on At-Home Dads," in *At-Home Dad Handbook,* http://slowlane.com/research/laymen_research.html (accessed March 23, 2002).
10. John M.Love, Peter Z. Schochet, and Alicia L. Meckstroth, "Are They in Any Real Danger? What Research Does—and Doesn't—Tell Us about Child Care Quality and Children's Well-Being," Mathematica Policy Research, Inc. (May 1996).
11. Ibid.
12. Center for the Child Care Workforce, "Current Data on Child Care Salaries and Benefits in the United States," Washington, DC (March 2002).
13. Ibid.

Chapter 2

1. Mark Lino, *Expenditures on Children by Families, 2001 Annual Report,* U.S. Department of Agriculture, Center for Nutrition Policy and Promotion, Alexandria, VA (2002): pp. 1528–2001.
2. Karen Schulman, "The High Cost of Child Care Puts Quality Care Out of Reach for Many Families," Children's Defense Fund, Washington, DC (2000).
3. Ibid.
4. Metro Transit web site, http://www.metrocouncil.org/transit/sprsvrs.htm (accessed November 7, 2002).
5. Ann Crittenden, *The Price of Motherhood: Why the Most Important Job in the World Is Still the Least Valued,* Metropolitan Books (2001).
6. Carmen DeNavas-Walt and Robert Cleveland, "U.S. Census Bureau, Current Population Reports, Money Income in the United States: 2001," U.S. Government Printing Office, Washington, DC (2002): pp. 60–218.
7. *The Columbia World of Quotations,* Columbia University Press (1996).
8. National Economic Council Interagency Working Group on Social Security, "Women and Retirement Security," (October 27, 1998).

Chapter 3
1.   Bridget Swinney, *Healthy Food for Healthy Kids,* Meadowbrook Press (1999): pp. 13, 21.
2.   Rachel K. Johnson and Theresa A. Nicklas, "Dietary Guidance for Healthy Children Ages 2–11 Years," position paper of the American Dietetic Association, *Journal of the American Dietetic Association,* 99 (1999): pp. 93–101.
3.   Penney E. McConnell and Jean B. Shaw, "Child and Adolescent Food and Nutrition Programs," *Journal of the American Dietetic Association,* 96 (1996): pp. 913–17.
4.   Ibid.
5.   Michael Jacobson and David Schardt, "Diet, ADHD, and Behavior: A Quarter Century Review," Center for Science in the Public Interest, Washington, DC (September 1999).
6.   American Academy of Pediatrics, *Guide to Your Child's Nutrition,* William H. Dietz and Loraine Stern, eds., Villard Books (1999): p. 205.
7.   "Breastfeeding and the Use of Human Milk," a policy statement reported in *Pediatrics,* 100:6 (December 1997): p. 1035.
8.   Christiane Northrup, *Women's Bodies, Women's Wisdom,* Bantam Books (1998): p. 506.
9.   Peggy O'Mara, *Natural Family Living: The Mothering Magazine Guide to Parenting,* Pocket Books (2000): p. 48.
10.   Christiane Northrup, *Women's Bodies, Women's Wisdom,* Bantam Books (1998): p. 506.
11.   Ibid.
12.   Marshall Klaus, "Mother and Infant: Early Emotional Ties," *Pediatrics,* 102:5 (November 1998): pp. 1244–46.
13.   American Academy of Pediatrics, *Guide to Your Child's Nutrition,* William H. Dietz and Loraine Stern, eds., Villard Books (1999).
14.   Rachel K. Johnson and Theresa A. Nicklas, "Dietary Guidance for Healthy Children Ages 2–11 Years," position paper of the American Dietetic Association. *Journal of the American Dietetic Association,* 99 (1999): pp. 93–101.
15.   American Academy of Pediatrics news release, February 23, 2000; original report in "Diabetes Care," *Journal of the American Diabetes Association,* 23:3 (March 2000): pp. 381–9.
16.   Bridget Swinney, *Healthy Food for Healthy Kids,* Meadowbrook Press (1999): pp. 6, 9–11.
17.   United States Department of Agriculture, "Tips for Using the Food Guide Pyramid for Young Children 2–6 Years Old," Center for Nutrition Policy and Promotion, Washington, DC (March 1999).
18.   Rachel K. Johnson and Theresa A. Nicklas, "Dietary Guidance for Healthy Children Ages 2–11 Years," position paper of the American Dietetic Association, *Journal of the American Dietetic Association,* 99 (1999): pp. 93–101.
19.   United States Department of Agriculture, "The Food Guide Pyramid,"

Home and Garden Bulletin, Center for Nutrition Policy and Promotion, Washington, DC, 252 (October 1996).

20. Tapan K. Basu, Norman J. Temple, and Manohar L. Garg, eds., *Antioxidants in Human Health and Disease,* CABI Publishing (1999): pp. 1, 249.

21. "The Many Powers of Fruits and Vegetables," *Wedge Coop Newsletter,* (August/September 2000): p. 2.

22. Judy McBride, "Can Foods Forestall Aging?" *Agricultural Research,* 47:2 (February 1999).

23. *Pesticides in the Diets of Infants and Children,* Committee on Pesticides in the Diets of Infants and Children, Board on Agriculture and Board on Environmental Studies and Toxicology, Commission on Life Sciences, National Research Council, National Academy Press, Washington, DC (1993): p. 1.

24. Ibid., pp. 23–24.

25. Brian P. Baker, et al., "Pesticide Residues in Conventional, IPM-Grown, and Organic Foods: Insights from Three U.S. Data Sets," *Food Additives and Contaminants,* 19:5 (May 2002): pp. 427–46.

26. C.Gärtner, W. Stahl, and H. Sies, "Lycopene Is More Bioavailable from Tomato Paste Than from Fresh Tomatoes," *American Journal of Clinical Nutrition,* 66 (July 1997): pp. 116–22.

27. Polly Berrien Berends, *Whole Child/Whole Parent,* HarperCollins (1997): pp. 216–36.

28. J. Madeline Nash, "Fertile Minds," *Time,* 3 (February 1997): p. 56.

29. Ibid., pp. 49–56.

30. Craig A. Anderson and Brad J. Bushman, "The Effects of Media Violence on Society," *Science,* 295 (March 29, 2002): pp. 2377–79.

31. Jane Healy, "Understanding TV's Effects on the Developing Brain," *AAP News* (May 1998).

32. U.S. Department of Health and Human Services, "The Surgeon General's Call to Action to Prevent and Decrease Overweight and Obesity," U.S. Department of Health and Human Services, Public Health Service, Office of the Surgeon General (2001).

33. D. B. Allison, et al., "Annual Deaths Attributable to Obesity in the United States," *Journal of the American Medical Association,* 282:16 (October 27, 1999): pp. 1530–38.

34. K. Kotz and M. Story, "Food Advertisements during Children's Saturday Morning Television Programming: Are They Consistent with Dietary Recommendations?" *Journal of the American Dietetic Association,* 94:11 (November 1994): pp. 1296–1300.

35. G.P. Sylvester, C. Achterberg, and J. Williams, "Children's Television and Nutrition: Friends or Foes?" *Nutrition Today,* 30:1 (January/February 1995): pp. 6–15.

36. K. Kotz and M. Story, "Food Advertisements during Children's Saturday Morning Television Programming: Are They Consistent with Dietary

Recommendations?" *Journal of the American Dietetic Association,* 94:11 (November 1994): pp. 1296–1300.

37. Katy Kelly, "False Promise," *U.S. News and World Report,* (September 25, 2000): pp. 49–55.

38. Ibid., p. 50.

39. Katherine Shaver, "Kids Have a Ride-Along Life," *Minneapolis Star Tribune* (March 10, 2003): p. E3.

40. Ibid.

41. Jerry Wyckoff and Barbara C. Unell, *Discipline without Shouting or Spanking,* Meadowbrook Press (2002): p. 3.

42. Ibid., p. 4.

43. Sarah Blaffer Hrdy, *Mother Nature,* Ballantine Books (1999): p. 212.

Chapter 4

1. Sarah Blaffer Hrdy, *Mother Nature,* Ballantine Books (1999): p. 90–91.

2. Ibid., p. 271.

3. Bridget Swinney, *Eating Expectantly,* Meadowbrook Press (2000): p. 162.

4. William J. Doherty, *Take Back Your Kids,* Sorin Books (2000).

5. Penny Simkin, Janet Whalley, and Ann Keppler, *Pregnancy, Childbirth, and the Newborn,* Meadowbrook Press (2001): p. 377.

6. Ibid.

7. Ibid., pp. 377–79.

8. Ibid., p. 380.

Chapter 5

1. Robert Frank, et al., "Primary Caregiving Father Families: Do They Differ in Division of Child Care and Housework?" http://slowlane.com/research/FAMJOU.html (accessed April 22, 2003).

Index

Also from Meadowbrook Press

✦ ***365 Baby Care Tips***
If babies came with an owner's manual, *365 Baby Care Tips* would be it. Packed full of the information new parents need to know—from teething, diapers, and breast- and bottle-feeding to discipline, safety, and staying connected as a couple—*365 Baby Care Tips* is the easy, essential guide to caring for a new baby.

✦ ***Busy Books***
The Children's Busy Book, The Toddler's Busy Book, The Preschooler's Busy Book and *The Arts and Crafts Busy Book* each contains 365 activities (one for each day of the year) for your children using items found around the home. The books offer parents and child-care providers fun reading, math, and science activities that will stimulate a child's natural curiosity. They also provide great activities for indoor play during even the longest stretches of bad weather! All four show you how to save money by making your own paints, play dough, craft clays, glue, paste, and other arts-and-crafts supplies.

✦ ***Discipline without Shouting or Spanking***
The most practical guide to discipline available, this newly revised book provides proven methods for handling the 30 most common forms of childhood misbehavior, from temper tantrums to sibling rivalry.

✦ ***Play and Learn***
Baby Play and Learn and *Preschooler Play and Learn*, from child-development expert Penny Warner, offer ideas for games and activities that will provide hours of developmental learning opportunities and fun for babies and young children. Each book contains step-by-step instructions, illustrations, and bulleted lists of skills your child will learn through play activities.

**We offer many more titles written to delight, inform, and entertain.
To order books with a credit card or browse our full
selection of titles, visit our web site at:**

www.meadowbrookpress.com

or call toll-free to place an order, request a free catalog, or ask a question:

1-800-338-2232

Meadowbrook Press • 5451 Smetana Drive • Minnetonka, MN • 55343